Bringing the Outside In

VISUAL WAYS TO ENGAGE RELUCTANT READERS

Sara B. Kajder

FOREWORD BY LINDA RIEF

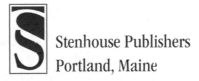
Stenhouse Publishers
Portland, Maine

Stenhouse Publishers
www.stenhouse.com

Copyright © 2006 by Sara B. Kajder

Library of Congress Cataloging-in-Publication Data

Kajder, Sara B., 1975–
    Bringing the outside in : visual ways to engage reluctant
readers / Sara B. Kajder; foreword by Linda Rief.
        p. cm.
    Includes bibliographical references.
    Contents: What does reading look like, anyway?—
Personal narrative and digital storytelling—Meeting a reader:
a literary narrative—Making a path through text—Working
with words—The visual think-aloud—Making meaning.
    ISBN 1-57110-401-1
    1. Reading (Secondary) 2. Reading—Remedial
teaching. 3. Visual learning. I. Title.

LB1632.K25 2006
428.4071'2—dc22   2005056415

Cover, interior design and typeset by studio 7 design

Manufactured in the United States of America on acid-free paper
11 10 09 08 07 06 9 8 7 6 5 4 3 2

To Karen Sinning, who taught me to really see my students.

*"The first step in transforming the world
is to begin to see it anew."*

John Willinsky, *The New Literacy*

CONTENTS

FOREWORD

Several years ago I had an 8th grader named Trapper. Because he was not doing well in my language arts class, and he wasn't offering much information about why the class wasn't working for him, I called in his parents to see what they could tell me. *Help me find his strengths. Tell me something about his learning style.* The information they offered was limited, but on the way out the door his mom turned and said, "Oh, has he ever mentioned the articles he writes for some Internet magazine? A cyberzine? I think that's what they call it." No, he hadn't, I told them, but I'd really be interested in seeing that writing.

It took more than a nudge to get him to bring several articles in to me. One of them, written for the International Mountain Bike Association Site, began this way:

> *A Guide to Suspension for Lighter Riders*
> *By Trapper S.*
>
> *The problem: Most forks come adjusted for riders that weigh 150–170 pounds, that means that anyone who weighs less than that will have to change the stock setup.*
>
> *The solution, tune your own fork to your needs. To start with, look for quick, supple elastomer forks. These forks are best for lighter riders because they suffer less stiction than hydraulic forks. In other words, they move much easier. . . .*

The article continued on for several more pages. Trapper's agreement with the cyberzine site? They would send him a mountain biking part to test out, he would write his findings, and get to keep the part as his "pay," whether it was a $35 or an $800 part.

In his quarterly evaluation of himself as a reader and writer, he wrote:

> *It all started about a year ago when I was cruising some mountain bike cyberzines on the internet. I came across the one web site that stood out from all the other cyberzines. I cruised the page for a couple of days. Then on the third day or so I found a spot where you could suggest ideas for articles or submit a description of yourself for a columnist. I sent my description in and made clear that I was 14 and had incredible bike knowledge and also had rather good writing ability. David Schloss sent me an e-mail saying what I had to do and I took it from there. I have written about ten stories for them and have just got an offer from another cyberzine called BikeSite.*
>
> *My reading is linked directly to what I write about. I literally study these magazines and specs on products, keep all the information in my brain for awhile (while I test out the part on my own bike at the same time.) I then let my brain sort and put all the pieces together to form an article . . . I then type these articles up and send them via e-mail to David Schloss, who then publishes them in his mountain bike cyberzine out of New Jersey. The cyberzine is published in over 60 countries and they have over 60,000 people on their mailing list. This is where my articles go once I hit the one button on my internet server, "send."*
>
> *I do actually read books, but what I mostly read are mountain bike magazines. I prefer* Mountain Bike *and* Mountain Bike Action. *In* Mountain Bike *I really enjoy the articles in the beginning of the issue written by Zapata Espinoza. He writes what's on his mind or what is the talk in the mountain bike world. I really like his articles because they're opinionated, unlike some other writers. Every night*

and morning I read/study these magazines for future articles that I will write in the future.

I will definitely send my resume into a mountain bike magazine as soon as I'm of reasonable age. I love writing, racing, and everything to do with mountain biking. I hope some day that I can write and ride like Zapata Espinoza.

Trapper would have flourished in Sara Kajder's class. What Sara shows us so thoroughly and clearly through this book is how she invites and *teaches* her students as readers "to visualize as they read, and to create and use visual tools to organize content, construct meaning, and analyze their processes and understanding." Trapper has done all of that. While Sara uses the tools of technology to engage readers in a visual experience that deepens their understanding of text, Trapper was literally using the actual visual (a mountain biking part), to construct meaning from his reading, for his understanding, to be explained in his writing.

Sara looks to these newer literacies as ways that allow her to "reach, engage, and move those students who aren't finding success in our classrooms." We cannot assume this book is focused on technology and not on "the basics." The book is about becoming a more effective reading teacher. Sara "challenges herself to find new ways to see her students, to value their literacies outside the classroom, and to lead them to see (and value) themselves as readers and writers inside the classroom." This book is a challenge to all of us as teachers to step into the twenty-first century along with our students. We need to catch up.

Why hadn't Trapper shown me what he was doing? Because he was doing it outside the classroom and didn't think "it counted." Sara introduces us to Rai, a student who carried around a sketchbook filled with his depiction of the school year in comic book format ("full of drawings, insights, satire, and honesty"), yet never considered it "English-stuff," worth sharing in the classroom. She introduces us to Ensui, who kept a Web log for himself as an ESL student, and Leah, who designed and produced a digital family video for her older brother who was headed to the Gulf. These are highly literate young men and women engaged in authentic reading and writing tasks outside the classroom, yet they never considered themselves successful as readers and writers *in* the classroom.

Sara's book illustrates, so artfully, the spaces she makes for these students, the ones who think their subject matter doesn't fit our content and the ones who have their own tools for communicating to others—sometimes *many* others—all they know and want to know more about. She wants learners to "tap into powerful communication tools to tell their story verbally, visually, and powerfully." And the book does just that by showing us as teachers how to use the tools of technology more meaningfully in our own classrooms in order to help all of our students—the struggling readers as well as the very able—show us who they are today as articulate, literate young men and women.

Sara explains *how* to use the tools of technology that already exist in most of our classrooms by designing experiences that teach us how to think like a reading teacher. What we have to remind ourselves constantly is that the focus *is* reading and writing. It is not the tool that delivers the meaning. Too often we take to heart the saying "the medium is the message." We cannot let technology be the message. It is there to enhance the message and make it easier to deliver, in the same way a word processor makes the typewriter obsolete. Yet, what we have to say matters more than what we use to say it. Sara shows us how to make the medium and the message matter.

I've always been intimidated by, and fearful of, technology, almost afraid to use it if I didn't know enough about it. Sara alleviates all that fear, while convincing us that we must know the tools because they do allow students, and their teachers, to do so many things better as readers and writers than what they could accomplish without the tools.

Through the concept of digital storytelling, visual read-alouds, and using images and logographic cues to mark our way through a text, she shows us how to use technology to learn, instead of learning a technology. In the process, however, we are learning the technology. Sara invites us to look at what students already know and use outside the classrooms, and then to reimagine—and she shows us—how to pair the texts, tools, and opportunities to immerse our students in real engagement. It is an invitation with detailed ideas into ways of thinking much more broadly and openly about how we define literary. It's about knowing our students and the real questions they bring to our classrooms. It's about teaching them how to become real problem-solvers by complicating and enriching their work as readers.

By using instructionally centered chapters Sara offers us student stories to ground our thinking, while discussing in each chapter some of "the dominant theory and thinking behind literacy instruction and how to teach reading."

She shows us how to make all that is visual about reading real to students. She clearly presents classroom ideas and strategies, giving us student exemplars to further our understanding. She grounds her thinking in the theories of sound researchers such as Anne Berthoff, whose work with representation holds that "visualizing, making meaning by means of mental images, is the paradigm of all acts of the mind. Students who learn to look and look again are discovering their powers."

After reading this book, I have to say I agree with Gus, one of Sara's students, whom she cites at the end of the book: "This is real reading. And I finally see what it looks like." As a teacher I too finally *see* what real reading looks like. Sara's book will help all of us as teachers guide our students to the same understandings.

Linda Rief
Oyster River Middle School
Durham, New Hampshire

Acknowledgments

The more that I learn, the more acutely aware I become of the great teachers who have shaped my thinking and experiences. Mr. Ross, Mrs. Lucas, Mr. Edelman, Dr. Tobias . . . You were the teachers who called out and "fed" my work as a writer, a reader, a thinker. You saw me—and I am grateful every day.

It has been several years since I learned to teach within her classroom, but I carry Karen Sinning's imprint into every classroom, every dialogue with colleagues, and every interaction with a student reader/writer. I aspire to being the kind of teacher that she is every day.

I am especially grateful to Dr. Glen Bull at the Center for Technology and Teacher Education at the University of Virginia whose relentless persistence in finding ways to engage student readers and writers with visual texts and stories started me down the path that has grown into this book.

Though we've come together through work at different schools and different times, I am so grateful to the community of talented teachers who continually push my thinking, invite me into their classrooms, and model what effective teachers do. Sandra Whitaker, Pat Harder, Melissa Boese, Molly Carter, Meredith Willey, Ashley Partin, Dr. Robyn Jackson, Kristin Shapira, Mary Wagner, Sarah Menke-Fish, Kathryn Lee—you're all present in these pages.

Thank you to my colleagues and mentors, especially Janet Swenson, Carol Tomlinson, Smokey Daniels, Kylene Beers, and Leila Christenbury for welcoming me to the conversation about what we can do to really move all kids as readers and writers. You've each challenged me in such valuable ways, many of which are reflected in this work. Thank you to Linda Rief for pushing me to articulate what really matters about bringing out-of-school literacies into our classrooms. Your questions have set me off on such important journeys.

I wouldn't have taken on the writing of this book had I not had the support and energy of Bill Varner behind each page. You are a scholar and a friend, and you somehow knew which of those voices to speak through at just the right time. I am very grateful.

I wrote this book while completing my studies in Virginia and taking on a new job and new life in Kentucky. It would never have been possible without the support of my family, and my husband, Michael. Thank you all for the support, time, and faith that helped me to juggle new roles and find unexpected joy in the balance. Rita, my mother-in-law, asked me each time we spoke whether or not I was writing. Thanks for making sure I was answering "yes."

Lastly, I owe a large thank-you to my son, Matthew, who has experienced his first year and a half of life as I have written this book. The day that I wrote the last word, you pulled up onto my lap with a book in tow. There is no better way to learn about reading than to experience it with you.

1: What Does Reading Look Like, Anyway?

Walking into third period Language Arts, I was met by thirty-five students who each read and wrote at a different level. We had less than thirty bedraggled copies of the "core" texts we'd be reading together, and sixteen copies of *Elements of Literature* anthologies were stacked on the shelves along the walls. There was one computer (a barely functioning Apple Classic IIE) in the rear corner of the room. In all honesty, it took no more than a couple of seconds to survey the "tools" at hand. It took significantly longer to dig into the literate lives of the students who made up our "community of learners" (to use the district's latest buzz-word).

These students were enrolled in the "on-level course." In other words, these were the students who weren't enrolled in an honors-level class or a standard-level class, where all students had successfully reached the required scores on the state reading assessment the year before. These were the students who might be reading below grade-level and be described as "reluctant" or "resistant." From the first day, many students put into play a series of sophisticated avoidance tactics such as rushing through tasks or working too slowly. Many had little or no tolerance for frustration. None of them were flexible readers. They were also tremendously frank in telling me on the first day of class that they were bored. Bottom line—these were students who hadn't met that test score the year before and who met my enthusiasm about working together as readers and writers with blank stares.

As I grew to know them, I was overwhelmed by who these students were as readers and writers outside of our classroom walls. EunSui maintained a Web log detailing his experiences as an ESL student that was widely read and received more hits in a day than our school site did in a month. Gerald, Ashley, and Amber were amazing photographers. Leah was compiling a family digital video to be shared when her older brother left to serve in the Gulf that November. Brit and Sam played PS2 games every afternoon, both against each other and also while tapped into a global network, interacting with players in an international field. Every student in the class had some interest that was anchored in authentic reading and writing; it was just something that lived well outside of our classroom, and something that hadn't yet led them to see themselves as uniquely and richly literate.

I was surprised, a little dismayed, and genuinely frustrated by how strongly these students resisted when I spoke to them as readers and writers. They wanted—no, they pleaded for—worksheets. They looked at me as if I were crazy when I talked about their out-of-school literacies as "counting." They didn't want to be seen. And, to use Tazik's words, they wanted me to "get real."

"GETTING REAL . . ."

Even before meeting these students, I strongly believed that literacy is much more than reading and writing print text, even though that is largely what we assess in school. As English teachers, we talk about literacy in multiple ways. We refer to functional literacy and emergent literacy, academic literacy and out-of-school literacy, oral literacy and visual literacy, alphabetic literacy and multi-modal literacy, critical literacy and cultural literacy. Equally wide is the range of new technologies that are changing the texts we create and consume and the cultural contexts in which they are shared. Through the use of these tools, we fuse image, color, words, and sound. We don't just rely on words to communicate. We use movement, space, the visual, and the auditory—and technologies provide new textual spaces for this reading, writing and thinking.

As English teachers, we are literacy teachers. We teach readers and writers, and use the spaces of our curricula and the literacy communities in our classrooms to move students to become better readers and writers. We teach in turbulent times—culturally, politically, and even within the terms that we use to define what it is that we lead students to do. Despite that, I believe that the ever-developing definition of what it means to be literate has a solid root—that literacy is using the most powerful cultural tools to communicate our understandings (Wilhelm 2001). That's where this book begins—in realizing and leveraging the almost exponentially increasing means of communication and leading all student readers to engage deeper with all forms of texts.

This book is really about my work in becoming a more effective reading teacher. It's about the ways in which I looked to the "newer" literacies as ways that would allow me to reach, engage, and move those students who weren't finding success. I believe firmly that my students' out-of-school literacies *do* count. What this work has done is challenge me to find new ways to see students, to value their literacies, and to lead them to see (and value) themselves as readers and writers inside our classroom spaces.

Meet Rai

Rai came to school an hour early each day, not because he was working with teachers or part of a club, but because if he caught a ride with his Dad, it was the single ten-minute span of time that he'd get to see him during the work week. Rai's Dad worked three jobs to keep the family afloat, leading him to leave home at 6:15 AM and return well after 10:30 PM, six days a week. In order to get those precious ten minutes, Rai rode in early, and spent the hour either catching up on homework, or, more regularly, sleeping in the corner of an open classroom.

He entered the classroom early one morning and came up to say his usual "Good morning," before heading to the reading corner where he typically rested until first period. I was engrossed in reading Anna Quindlen's *How Reading Changed My Life,* and only looked up when I heard Rai's sigh. I quickly greeted him.

"Ah, Ms. Kajder. Reading hasn't changed my life for nothin' better."

With that, he trudged off to the reading corner. Bells and whistles were erupting in my teacher-brain, as I realized that there was so much to untap in his story.

I probed. I asked him to talk with me about his experiences as a reader. I asked how reading had impacted his school life, his time at home, his play . . . He had little more than one-word "nah" and "dunno" answers for me—and this was a kid who was usually much more articulate, even at this early hour. Was it possible that he simply didn't have the words to talk about his reading?

And then, I remembered the digital camera sitting on my desk. I asked Rai to take the camera with him, and to return the next morning with a picture that represented what he knew and believed about reading. He agreed, returning the next morning with the following photo:

FIGURE 1.1: RAI'S PHOTO OF A BULLDOZER

He then proceeded to talk for forty-five minutes about how reading was about tearing things apart, and only rebuilding once he had plans from a teacher or more skilled reader. He used the photo to represent his thinking, but he also used it to re-present his ideas.

Rai sought out this kind of visual work. In opening his ideas about reading through our discussion of this single image, Rai also took a bigger step—he opened up his backpack and pulled out a sketchbook in which he'd been depicting the entire school year as a comic book. The pages were full of drawings, insights, satire, and honesty. When I asked him why he'd never brought this work into our classroom discussions or even journaling time, he quickly insisted, "This isn't English stuff, Ms. Kajder. It doesn't count. It's just play."

I was overwhelmed. Here was this intensely bright, talented reader and writer who had so much to bring to our literacy community and who felt that his modes of expressing and making meaning weren't valued in the one class that's about making a space for authentic and engaged reading and writing.

MEET GUS

I met Gus just as his tenth-grade English class was beginning its study of *To the Lighthouse.* He was a gregarious, vocal student whose glasses and habitually mussed hair were just enough of a visual cue for his peers to call him "Harry" or "Potter." I observed the class as they completed anticipation guides and some situational role-plays meant to help students activate their prior knowledge and become prepared to enter the text. After forty-seven minutes, the class bell rang, and students began to collect their books and head out. In the midst of my note taking, I saw that Gus, now filing out the door, had left his copy of the novel sitting on his desk.

"Hey, Gus!" I called. "Forget something?"

"Nope," he shrugged.

I held up his copy of the text as he made his way back to his desk.

"It's going to be hard to read this tonight if it's sitting on your desk," I joked.

"Ah, no worries. I don't do that," he offered.

The look on my face was apparently enough to trigger his response.

"Oh, no. Don't worry. I'll get a B. I just don't read the book."

Again, my face triggered a response.

"Here's what it is . . . I don't read books. I do all we do in class, and pick up a lot. I talk to the gang in here that does read, and pick up some more. I go online. But, be real. When I want to read, this isn't it."

"So, what *is* it?" I asked.

Gus furled his brow, apparently surprised that I'd asked (and more than likely wondering how he was going to make it to his next class on time—a situation I addressed silently by beginning to write him a pass.)

"I don't know . . . I read the paper in the morning. I read articles and guides on PS3. I read what I get when my friends text me. I read a ton of blogs, but I aggregate them or else it would take scads of time . . . I go there for the cheats . . . I used to read liners of CD's, but now I just read online because I download MP3's from iTunes. I had to read my car manual last night because one of the lights got busted. But, I know that stuff doesn't count."

"What do you mean?" I asked.

"It's not reading. I don't know what to call it, but you'll never see a teacher assign or discuss anything like that. I can use that stuff, ya know? It's work that I'm wired to do—not like in here. I mean, what does reading look like, anyway?"

As Gus went on to his third-period class, I thought about what he'd said. As a reader, he read authentically and purposefully. He was reading selectively and critically, evaluating online gaming sites and blogs. His reading involved multiple genres and modalities. He was savvy enough to know how to navigate in-class tasks, but he needed to be drawn into higher-order tasks that addressed texts as tools for learning. And clearly, his perception of his own competency as a reader was impacting his work in this classroom. Gus was a reader. Just not in the English classroom . . .

THE READING CRISIS

Students like Gus and Rai enter our classrooms during a time labeled as a crisis in adolescent literacy. Over the past few years, we've seen a proliferation of reports and mandates, and have begun to feel the real impact of the No Child Left Behind Act on our classroom work. Where there are many who offer counter-arguments and counter-lenses to the numbers coming from NAEP data (Allington 2006), some of the numbers have strongly influenced how I think about literacy and my work with middle school and high school readers. Consider the following:

- More than half of students entering high school in the thirty-five largest cities in the United States read at the sixth-grade level, or below (deLeon 2002, p. 2).

- There are approximately eight million struggling readers in grades 4–12 (NCES 2003).

- 70 percent of older readers require some form of remediation. Very few of these older struggling readers need help to read the words on the page; their most common problem is that they are not able to comprehend what they read (Biancarosa and Snow 2004, p. 8).

- Less than 6 percent of our high school seniors can effectively monitor their comprehension, identify main ideas, support their readings with evidence from a text, and/or infer implied relationships (NCES 2003).

- At grade 8, the average score gaps on the NAEP reading assessment in 2003 between white and black students and between white and Hispanic students did not differ significantly from those in 2002 or 1992 (Donahue, Daane, and Grigg 2003).

- More than three thousand students drop out of high school every day (Alliance for Excellent Education 2003).

There is much to consider with each of these numbers and statistics, but looking at them together told a story that helped me to see into the realities of my classroom. To be perfectly honest, I had often wondered if it was just me—just my readers—just my classroom—just my teaching. These problems are an increasing reality across all of our classrooms, a reality that demands critical thinking about who we teach, what we teach, and how we teach in order to move *all* our kids. That's what good teachers do.

We need to consider and engage the readers we don't reach. In my classroom, I interact with students who could be described as "struggling readers" (Beers 2003) daily. But, I see something different in Gus and Rai, and the majority of the students in my classes who aren't finding success. First, these are students who are honestly surprised when I ask them to think about themselves as readers. They don't see themselves as a part of the practice or community within our classroom. For some, this is about confidence; for others, it's about the role that literacy and reading have played in life outside of school.

The reality is that most students struggle as readers when engaging with complex, rich texts. However, those students who fall into the 70 percent discussed in the *Reading Next* report (Biancarosa and Snow 2003) are the students who don't know how to deploy strategies to work through texts when they become "stuck." In my classroom, these are usually students who read without questions or a purpose in mind; they passively expect the text to work on them as opposed to expecting to take action themselves. However, the resistant or reluctant readers in my classroom know how to do this kind of work when reading an image or writing a Web log entry. When we acknowledge their out-of-school literacies and provide them with a space to exercise them in our classrooms, an opportunity emerges to bridge those texts and to invite these students into the "literacy club."

"WHAT DOES READING LOOK LIKE, ANYWAY?"

As I closely considered Gus's question, I was surprised by how difficult it was to answer. Flashes of literary theory and moments from my own experiences were the first line of response. I had been taught as a student that reading was about making sounds out of letters, making words out of letters, and then constructing sentences (and perhaps some meaning) out of those words. My English teachers read through a New Critical lens, which meant that I was continually reading for the meaning that was buried deep within the text. Reading became one part scavenger hunt and one part "read the mind of the teacher in the front of the room."

I also considered the piles of books and lists of bookmarked online materials that I was reading—and what I had recently read about what "counts" as real reading. A copy of the 2004 *Reading at Risk* report released by the National

Endowment for the Arts had just been sent to me by a colleague in Maryland. In reading it, I was presented with a genuinely dark view of the decline of reading's role within our culture. Within a week of the release of the report, I found myself reading a relative explosion of articles and editorials, many echoing and amplifying the alarm.

As an active and even voracious reader, I expected to see myself in the numbers who were counted as dedicated readers. Instead, I found myself reading the report in an attempt to find a single place where I could "live" as a reader. I'm a voracious reader of newpapers, non-fiction, Web sites, Web logs, professional texts, photography, and short stories. I'll delve into novels when I feel them beckon, but on a daily basis, I'm more likely to read other kinds of texts. The study defines literary reading tightly, offering that "literary reading is the reading of novels, short stories, poetry or drama in any print format, even the Internet" (2). Here I was, a professor and teacher of English teachers, and, just like Rai and Gus, I was clearly not a member of the literacy club.

Neither the definitions of reading that grew out of my experiences as a student nor those offered here by the NEA hold up when I think about the way that reading lives within my classroom, and especially not in the way that it lives within Rai's or Gus's practices as readers. I don't learn how to read by doing drills or listening to the reading offered by the lecturer in the front of the room. I continue to learn how to read by reading. As Krashen writes, "reading for meaning, reading for things that matter to us, is the cause of literate language development" (p. 85).

That means that reading in my classroom doesn't look like what Steven described in his eighth-grade class reflection at the start of the school year:

> *I watch the kids in the classroom—the smart kids and the ones that are more like me. I look down at the page, but not far enough so that I can't see where they are. Once they turn the page, I tap my foot eight beats, and then turn my page. If I went faster or slower, that would call attention to where I was. This way, I look like I'm reading, but I'm really counting.*

He called this his reader's choreography. It also isn't like Katerina's experiences as noted in her reader's journal:

> *The worst part about reading is reading. I slog through. Funny thing is that I read all that is assigned, but I don't remember anything that I read.*

Reading needs to be an engaging and powerful experience, but it doesn't come unless we teach students how. I don't expect every student to enter the classroom as a good reader, but I expect our classroom to be a place where he or she gets to be a better reader. Part of that means that I explicitly say to all students that good readers don't always zip through the pages, they regularly re-read, write while they read, re-read again, and often leave a text with many more questions than they had before they started.

If reading is the ability to decode alphabetic texts, then the research cited earlier tells us that the majority of secondary readers are already there. So, reading instruction for those students doesn't "look" like it did when I was a student: English-classroom specific instruction on phonics (matching letters to sounds), then practice with fluent oral reading (reading aloud), and then work on comprehension. Instead, it takes on a strategy focus, offering students models, practice, and application before, during, and after reading.

Students have choice in the books that they read, with required texts unifying the class and allowing us to discuss, construct meaning from, and write about great literature. And, of course, we use technology to access and construct texts that are multigenre, multimedia, and multimodal and to then convey our understanding to a variety of audiences.

In working with student readers at all levels and from all backgrounds, it's helped me to see reading in four "categories":

QUICK READING	CRITICAL READING	MINDFUL READING	ORBITAL READING
A reader is dipping into the text, working to decode, but also working bigger, looking to get a sense of the subject or, possibly, a rough sense of its meaning.	A reader works to, as my students put it, "interrogate the text." This is reading to understand meaning but also to examine how literary elements are used and how the text was crafted.	When a reader approaches a text to conduct mindful reading, he or she is reading to learn and understand. The reader uses that new knowledge to complete a task or learn something new about himself or herself.	Carol Tomlinson taught me this term. This is what happens when readers read across texts. Reading evokes connections to other texts, and leads the reader to think about patterns as well as ideas.

Once I started sharing this with my students, it was interesting to see how it not only drew out their stories and experiences as readers but how it disengaged anxieties that they brought to our in-class reading. When I first wrote it (on a board in the back of the classroom), it was more of a hierarchy, leading students to think that "good" reading happened only at the "orbital stage."

By organizing it horizontally, students were more able to see that these were different kinds of reading as opposed to stages of a process.

MULTI-LITERACIES AND REMEDIATION

When I think about Gus's question, I think a great deal about the texts that he *did* read, texts that push me to broaden my thinking to include print, visual, digital and various other modalities. As I discussed earlier, the definition of "literacy" seems to be almost constantly in flux as texts, tools, and tasks change. The New London Group (1996, p. 62) defined literacy as "the understanding and competent control of representational formats that are becoming increasingly significant in the overall communications environment, such as visual images and their relationship to the written word—for instance, visual design in desktop publishing or the interface of visual and linguistic meaning in multimedia." Visionary—and yet, already dated. Gus was talking about blogs and online texts. As you read this, there will very likely be other media and modes to consider. However, the message remains a constant. Students don't just read; they read in a specific time and place, and for a deliberate purpose. That demands that we open our curricula to include new options.

As much as this book will do that by incorporating visual and digital texts (and the means for sharing them with broader audiences), we also need to consider an instructional framework that helps to take this even further. "Remediation," as described and defined by Luke and Elkins (2000), challenges teachers and students to incorporate a broadened definition of text to include those that are multimodal—visual, auditory, digital, or spatial. We know that the literacies students exercise outside of our classrooms are different from those that are school-recognized, to the point that the literature base is filled with references to academic literacies vs. out-of-school literacies. One central aspect of my work is the belief that by using multiple forms of text, we can scaffold students into successful interactions with more academic, print-based literacy. And, more importantly, we can lead students to see themselves as successful readers and writers who can construct, analyze and compose using a variety of modes and media.

I was trained to view remediation as a means of reteaching content and moving the skills of students who weren't successful at the first go. With remediation, I need to critically consider ways of moving the skills of all my students by teaching with a broader range of multimodal, multimedia texts. I still hold tightly to my treasured literary texts. However, I lead students through different paths to access them, and we read them in dialogue with texts that incorporate movement, space, the visual, and the auditory. This requires seeing my students and attending closely enough to them that I see a new and very real way to pair texts, tools, and opportunities for authentic engagement.

AND TECHNOLOGY?

Here's what this book won't offer you. We won't be exploring or discussing ways to teach with the flood of packaged literacy programs that are often all that are considered when it comes to using technology to teach reading. We also aren't going to discuss software programs that are designed to help improve decoding, spelling, fluency, and vocabulary.

When we talk about technologies, we'll address those multi-media, multi-modal authoring tools which already exist in most classrooms: a minimum of one classroom computer (PC or Mac), a digital camera, and authoring tools like PowerPoint or Keynote (multimedia presentation software), Photoshop or iPhoto (photo-editing software), and digital video editing tools like MovieMaker or iMovie.

Why? I believe in teaching students how to mindfully use, author with, and critically evaluate the most powerful cultural tools we have for communicating meaning. I don't believe that you learn that by keying in "a, b, c, or d" in response to a multiple-choice test, or by watching flash animations that illustrate a cartoon character's adventures through word-land. I want all of my students to read and write for authentic purposes. That means developing and exercising real literacies.

This book won't teach you how to use those software tools, but it will teach you how to think with them like a reading teacher. There are two guiding questions essential to the work ahead:

1. What are the unique capacities of this tool? (i.e., What can I do with it that I can't do with anything else?)

2. What does it allow me to do that's better (instructionally) than what I could do without it?

The tools that we have available for this type of composing and meaning making are going to change—probably within the life of this book, and absolutely within the life of our teaching careers. However, those two essential questions will remain the same and will remain valuable tools to help keep your thinking focused on teaching and how to move students.

Simply put, the strategies in this book require only that you are able to think openly and broadly about what we define as text and what we define as literacy. In critically considering the multiple modes, media, and means at our disposal in relation to our students' needs and skills as readers and writers, we create infinite possibilities for where our classrooms can lead.

I also want to be really open about the skills that you need in order to implement these strategies. You need to be open to knowing your students. You need to be open to thinking about reading and writing instruction in some new ways. That's it. I don't expect you to be a techie. Some of these strategies will involve a pen or pencil, "old-school" technologies that are an essential and transparent part of our toolkit. Some will involve more sophisticated tools, all of which I had to wrestle with in order to figure out how they could meaningfully contribute to the work we conduct in our classrooms. This book will model that thinking process so that when the tools change, you'll know how to lift your thinking to utilize new capacities.

The root remains the same—we'll think about the genuine instructional questions and problems that live in our classrooms, and then problematize the ways that the unique capacities of the tools allow us to work toward answering them. We won't be focused on iMovie "basics" because iMovie most likely won't be a dominant tool later on down the road. However, the ability to think about how to best use the tool to inform, guide, and move student learning will, hopefully, still remain at the center of what we do.

WHERE WE'RE HEADED

The instructionally centered chapters in this book all follow the same format. They begin with a student's story to anchor our inquiry and discuss some of the dominant theory and thinking behind literacy instruction and how we teach reading. This leads to classroom ideas and strategies, student exemplars and, lastly, additional ideas and reflection. This isn't a static text, but one that is meant to challenge you to continually rethink and grow, no matter where you start. It aims at establishing a space for you to think about your classroom philosophies and practices while acting as a catalyst to push you to sample new strategies and ways of thinking. It is my hope that you transform the ideas and strategies to utilize your resources to richly impact all the student readers in your classrooms.

Lastly, this text is accompanied by a Web site (www.bringingtheoutsidein. com), which I maintain as a place for our continued discussion and to share additional strategies, research and ideas. As the students, texts, and technologies which fill our classrooms continually change and develop, this Web site will allow us to maintain what is "current" while the philosophies and dialogues in the text continue to root our thinking about how we teach all students to become better readers.

Let's get started . . .

2: Personal Narrative and Digital Storytelling

Hanging on the door of room 173 is a black-and-white photograph of the door to my grandmother's house. Students regularly question its placement and content, as most of the doors down the hall are either covered with construction paper (so others cannot see in) or covered with flyers announcing school events. I reply simply, "It's an invitation."

Sometimes I am prompted to share a story about that door, about why the photo shows it half-open and how that makes me feel secure and welcome. Sometimes I ask students what they see in the door, asking them to consider how it might be a part of what they know. No matter what story I share, it is paired with an opening (much like that door), invoking and evoking students' stories and welcoming them into our shared learning space.

Stories abound in this classroom, allowing students to see themselves in our work, to participate within our literacy community and, often, to take huge strides in defining themselves as readers and writers. In a culturally diverse, socioeconomically challenged suburban school ten minutes from Washington, D.C., the mix of students is rich and staggering. The thirty-seven students in period two, English 11, were the first to tell me that they were not readers or writers—and their test scores and student files reflected several years of that thinking. I countered that they were. Each time they picked up a manual, jumped online to instant message (IM) a friend, or got on the Metro and headed into town, they were readers. Culturally, there is an argument that holds that the competition for reading as a source of stories has become more intense. It proposes that students are captivated by the Internet, television, film, and video games *instead* of reading. I believe that these media support and *promote* reading. These students are intensely literate but not in the ways that might allow them to score well on tests.

Early into our first semester, I "reinvented" a unit on personal narrative, working to evoke students' stories, extend their literacy skills, and provide a multimedia environment that allowed them to work not only as readers and writers but also as directors, artists, programmers, screenwriters, and designers. As a culminating activity, students created a digital story that conveyed a 3–5 minute personal narrative in response to a significant question and experience of each student's choosing. The project took two weeks of instructional time and required the development of a sustained community.

It was not an easy sell. Students lacked trust, rarely having space within a classroom that was their own. They all read below level and were accustomed to worksheets as opposed to invitations to be heard and seen. We started with the reality Adrienne Rich describes, "When someone with the authority of a teacher describes the world and you are not in it, there is a moment of psychic disequilibrium, as if you looked into a mirror and saw nothing" (1979, p. 36). Each student had to look into the mirror and see through different eyes.

Rochelle's story spoke to and about her mother. Their relationship was strained and had led to Rochelle's rebellion in the form of many piercings and detentions. Rochelle was a student with tremendous capacity who just did not see where to start. We began this project in late September, and it was the first piece of writing that Rochelle submitted. Expecting our routine struggle when it came time to collect her work, I was stunned when Rochelle entered class, submitted a rather tattered first draft of her script, and smiled.

In what grew into a three-and-a-half-minute digital story, Rochelle's voice told the story of her mother riding a streamer-laden pink bike down the dirt paths that were the initial construction sites for I-270. The images rotated from black-and-white shots of her mother at age fifteen to those of a grinning, six-year-old Rochelle in brilliant color, riding her own bike with her mother trailing close behind. Taking full advantage of images that spoke, she balanced the use of her voice with moments where silence allowed the image to communicate. She closed with the words, "I would have liked to have known the girl with the wind in her hair."

This was Rochelle's entrance into our interpretive community. Not every day was a great day, but several marked triumphs in her work as a reader and a writer. She explained in a journal entry late in the year, "We started class with where I was instead of starting with everything I didn't know and because of that, I'm starting to know where to begin." That same day, Rochelle placed a sign underneath the image of my grandmother's door. It read, "Enter Here."

WHAT IS DIGITAL STORYTELLING?

In an early class discussion exploring the compelling qualities and nature of storytelling, Rochelle shared that "stories capture our voices telling our own stories." This is just what a digital story is—the melding of human voice and personal narrative, using technologies only as tools that bring these elements together into one text. Digital storytelling grew out of the work of Dana Atchley, Joe Lambert, and the Center for Digital Storytelling at University of California at Berkeley in 1993. Joe often explains in the workshops held at the center that "the digital story is more like film for the rest of us." Good stories require honesty and simplicity, not the skills of a great auteur or a techie. My students saw our work as the work of the storyteller, with the computer working only as a tool for eventual publication and sharing. Or, as Elliot explained in his journal, "we aren't learning a technology; we're using a technology to learn."

Lambert identifies seven elements of effective digital stories, which helped to fuel much of our work: Point of View, Dramatic Question, Emotional Content, Voice, Soundtrack, Pacing and Economy (Lambert 2002). I like to group these elements, focusing on their use and importance "during writing" and "during construction" elements (see Table 2.1).

Point (of View)

Students' digital stories need to be built from their own experience and understanding, using "I" as opposed to a more distant third person point of view. However, I place "of view" in parentheses in an attempt to signal the importance of the "point" of the story. Good stories take us somewhere. Every part of the story works toward a "point" which evokes some response from the audience. This focus is useful for student writers, especially those in my classroom who often wrote for pages without knowing where they were going.

TABLE 2.1: ELEMENTS OF A DIGITAL STORY

DURING WRITING	DURING CONSTRUCTION
Point (of view)	Soundtrack
Dramatic Question	Pacing
Emotional Content	Economy
Voice	

Dramatic Question and Emotional Content

Effective stories do more than work toward a point. Narratives that lead the reader to become invested typically pursue a compelling question that evokes interest and commitment, and sets the reader up for the eventual "payoff" at the close of the story. This was extremely challenging for my student writers who would either bury the question too deeply in the story or whose story structure fished around for a question. Only through revision and story circle activities (discussed later in this chapter) did students begin to shape their stories into a text that rewarded and surprised their readers and viewers.

Voice

This class of thirty-seven had several "unheard" and "unseen" students. They might enter the classroom, submit work, and leave at the sound of the bell without participating in discussion, group assignments, or any task that asked for their voices. The process of digital storytelling required that students exercise their voices as writers and as readers, sharing their drafts in a story circle that aimed at eliciting helpful, reflective peer responses to the text when read aloud. Further, students must absolutely record themselves narrating their scripts—a process that paralyzed even my most vocal students. They are the storytellers, reading (not reciting) their own words, their own ideas, and their own stories. Although it's the largest obstacle at the start of the process, it's often the most empowering element of the experience. As Ron explained in a reflective exit ticket after we viewed his class's stories, "Reading stories made me hear things in my voice. Seeing stories let me hear people in this class in a whole other way."

Soundtrack

We address soundtrack late in the construction process, emphasizing to students that there is a power to placing instrumental music under their voices and images as the story unfolds. I'm continually surprised by students' skills when it comes to selecting and cuing music that allows them to take their intended meaning to a different, more powerful level. Where a colleague of mine argues that this makes the story a music video, students find that sound adds complexity and depth to the narrative. This also provides students with a lesson in music copyright that in an era of file sharing and Kazaa.com seems more and more pressing.

Pacing

I remember many childhood hours sitting up with my father, whose stories would unfold with a rhythm and energy that led me to cling to each word he spoke. That's the art of the storyteller, made even more essential as students work within a digital space to compile and communicate their stories. In my notes from a digital storytelling workshop led by the team at the Center for Digital Storytelling, I have written in all caps and underlined the phrase "GOOD STORIES BREATHE." Pacing is all about letting that happen. For student writers, this means pulling back or racing forward when the story calls for it, as opposed to when the time limit approaches.

Economy

I think that this is one of the most essential elements when students are working with digital multimedia. Too often, we're led to add effects and bells and whistles because the tool is capable of it or because it helps us to replicate the visual onslaught that we see on MTV or even CNN. I argue to students that the effective digital story uses only a few images, a few words, and even fewer special effects to clearly and powerfully communicate intended meaning. Here, students need to work to include only what's necessary as opposed to what's possible.

INTO THE CLASSROOM

Getting Started: Prewriting, Reading and Thinking Tasks

In designing the unit, I quickly realized that there were several significant ideas that I needed to introduce and discuss with students if I were to build on their skills and capacities as readers and writers. First, we needed to define what it meant to be literate. To Joscisa and Sahar, it meant "the ability to read and to write what you're thinking." Niko countered that literacy was "all the stuff that we don't learn in school that allows us to be who we are." Tamyra offered that "literacy is about knowing what tool I need to use to share my thoughts." Together, we agreed that literacy requires knowing how and when to use "the most powerful cultural tools for making, communicating and conveying meaning" (Wilhelm, Baker, and Dube 2001, p. 12). Today, that includes online technologies, communication technologies and tools (like email or IM), and software tools that allow us to visualize thinking and represent it in multiple ways.

Our second big idea targeted story. Students shared and discussed family stories, books from their childhood (though only three of thirty-seven students had actual "artifacts" to share), and stories about their experiences in school. As I crafted the lessons and activities, I was driven by Langer's idea that "all literature—the stories we read and those we tell—provides us with a way to imagine human potential" (Langer 1995, p. 5). Students were sounding their stories and balancing them against the authors we read (Frank McCourt, Anne Lamott, Alice Walker, Maxine Hong Kingston, Lucy Grealy, Gary Soto, and others) in an attempt to validate, understand, and problematize their experiences. Bruner writes that "language is a way of sorting out one's thoughts about things" (1986, p. 74), and story provided an entrance into writing for those students who wrestled with putting the right words together to communicate exactly what they wanted to express.

As writers, students were actively working as readers of their written text and the writing of their peers, and exercising new muscles as they took on the published texts in our curriculum. We know that students are more motivated when they are given the choice and the latitude to include texts that interest them (Ivey 2000). In working with story and personal narrative, these formerly unmotivated readers dove into the bookcases and read actively in the library after school.

Equipped with strategies we had modeled and explored in class, students struggled to find entrances but did not quit. As Lashawna put it, "writing that's real and that matters" challenged student comprehension in the sense that Harvey means when she writes that "comprehension means that readers think not only about what they are reading but what they are learning" (2000, p. 9). Students read not to glean what the color green meant in a text but what significance that story had to their own understanding and experience. Reading, both in and outside of the classroom, is about much more than simply absorbing words on a page. As Gallas writes, "to read a text with understanding and insight, we must move inside a text, pulling our life along with us and incorporating the text and our lives into a new understanding of the world" (2003, p. 20). The combination of story and student interest allowed me to challenge students to demonstrate that they knew what to do with texts beyond just saying the words.

I felt the need to consider our district's idea of "rigor," knowing that the task would be challenged by some in the building who argued that student choice was a curricular luxury when working with lower-level students or that technology integration was about play as opposed to learning. Rigor is about challenging students to learn in new, evocative, and meaningful ways. Myers writes that "learning is not about transmitting or acquiring knowledge ... it's about transformation" (1996, p. 27). Students were not reading for information. They were reading to relate, to connect, and to understand. Further, this was a task steeped in connections, a requirement for learning, as Dyson explains:

> *Children must link new material to old material, with its familiar frames of relationships and purposes; without such linkages they cannot approach the new with any sense of agency, with any sense at all. Old information must be recontextualized within and transferred to new systems of relationships and uses ... as new material enters into and transforms old relational rhythms, and old material reverberates in the new. (1999, p. 162)*

New understanding shaped and drove a revision of former ideas and practices. Content and writing drove this assignment. The technology was simply a delivery tool that ultimately provided a hook to tap into students' existing visual and technological literacies.

The Task at Hand: Crafting the Story

Nuts and Bolts

In a district curriculum packed with required tasks designed to address local and state standards, we had two weeks (five instructional ninety-minute blocks) to work with personal narrative, excite student reading, incite student writing, and lead them through the process of creating a finished digital story. We didn't know whether or not we could realistically bring it all together and filled each class, lunch, and after-school period to the brim. As long as students were willing to work, I was willing to make the tools available. This was not a school or a classroom with abundant technological tools. We worked with five outdated iMac computers (two in our classroom and three housed next door), running an early version of iMovie. (Newer operating systems come with digital video editors bundled in—iMovie in OSX for Mac and Windows MovieMaker in Windows XP.) We learned iMovie together as I raided the shelves of the local bookstore for manuals and guidebooks and as students navigated their way through the somewhat intuitive interface. Further, this was an experience that required me to work as a coach, recognizing that the development of the

MANAGING THE TECHNOLOGY

Many of the teachers that I work with are blocked by their lack of technology skills. In working with this unit, I, too, was essentially learning alongside my students. We used digital video editing tools because we could—but PowerPoint has similar capacity to fuse images alongside sound.

What's essential here isn't that you are the master of the technology tools. Yes, this should not be the very first time that you open the software. You need at least some familiarity with the basic functions of the tool (opening documents, saving materials, working with a timeline) in order to help students troubleshoot and structure the time spent in the classroom. And yes, you might need to provide students with some reference materials. However, there is an advantage in that the software is extremely intuitive and students bring a visual acuity that will surprise you.

students' work would be a dynamic, non-prescribed process. Our two weeks played out as follows:

Step One: Prewriting (What do I have to say?)

Students worked through several stages of construction after a reading scramble and full-class discussion on the differences between personal narrative and memoir. First, they needed to identify specific stories "worth telling." This was initially problematic, as students struggled against the voice of an internal editor who argued that their stories were not worth sharing. Several exercises helped:

1.   Students drew a detailed map of the neighborhood in which they grew up. This included the layout of the streets, homes of friends and strange neighbors, location of school, location of local hangouts, and so forth (Roorbach 1998, pp. 21–34).

2.   In a journal exercise, students were asked to respond to the following: "Think of your favorite childhood coat. What is in your pockets?"

3.   In another journal exercise, students were asked to respond to the following: "Write about a decisive moment (one where you ended up heading in an unanticipated direction) in your life."

The results were surprising. Students understood that the personal narrative needed to be a window into a moment, a self-contained story set in one particular place and time. They chose to tell rich stories that were about discovery and understanding. Dahabo, an immigrant from Somalia, wrote the story of the first day she wore pants, explaining what freedom and America meant to her. Niko wrote about seeking his first job, wanting security and possibility, or, to use his words, "the ceiling of America and the floor of Greece, my family's home." Though they were all locked in on the logistics of writing, each student submitted a draft of between one and one-and-a-half pages, double-spaced. The length was short but required packed, precise language and provided an entrance for struggling writers who were intimidated by the blank page. The trick was to develop voice while exercising economy.

Step Two: Artifact Search

Students' digital stories were built from an assortment of still images. I had assumed that this would be the simplest part of the process, but it was actually the most difficult. Students simply did not have photos to use. We used a Parent-Teacher-Student Association mini-grant to purchase disposable cameras that students could take home to photograph the places and objects that would help to tell their stories. The media center specialist also allowed students to check out the school digital camera (a three-year-old Sony Mavica acquired with "Apples for Students" money). Students also worked with print images, scanning or creating a "copy" by photographing each with the digital camera. This was a quick process, as most student movies used less than fifteen images.

Step Three: Storyboarding

Students were required to map on paper each image, technique, and element of their story by constructing a storyboard. This visual story had two dimensions: chronology—what happens and when—and interaction—how audio information interacts with the images (Lambert 2002, p. 61). Using a template supplied by the Center for Digital Storytelling, students arranged and rearranged images that were listed on sticky notes. The storyboard also required the writer to consider how effects, transitions, and sound would be sequenced. I conferenced with students, reviewing the finished storyboard and using it as an "entrance ticket" to use a classroom computer. Students worked at different paces and the instructional time was scaffolded and individualized, allowing some students to work with the assigned reading while others worked to construct their stories.

Step Four: The Story Circle

Students needed a place in which they could discuss what they were getting right in their work and those areas that needed additional development. They needed a place in which they could practice the pacing and sound of reading aloud. They also needed a place to take some risks, hear their own stories, and work as a community to develop ideas further. To that end, we introduced the

QUESTIONS TO SPUR THE CONVERSATION

As skilled as we are at leading discussions, leading student writers to develop their digital stories can be a challenge. What follows are questions that have proven to be effective in helping student writers to consider and develop their scripts:

- *Why tell this story now?*

- *Consider the images that you're going to use within the story. Are there places where they can do the heavier narrative work, and you can pull back on your words?*

- *Who is your intended audience?*

- *What do you see happening on the screen at this point in the story? How do the images and the words work together?*

- *What's the most important moment (or even sentence) in the script? What happens if we just start there?*

"story circle" as a time for sharing drafts, developing ideas, and supporting one another through the work of expressing a compelling story.

Because of the size of the class, we broke into three circles, each of which was facilitated by an English teacher from the school who was on a planning period. I circulated between circles in order to support, add comments, and get a sense of the evolving conversations and energy. Initially, we worked with volunteers, asking them to read the script aloud and then respond to comments which were all framed with the prompt "If this were my story, I . . ." Students, at first, needed to be drawn into the community, through their eyes and their voices. However, once the second or third script was read, a momentum began to unfold and the room filled with comments and ideas. Teacher-faciliators reached a point where we needed to monitor feedback only to ensure we didn't overwhelm student readers with the volume of responses. Readers took notes on their drafts and worked to implement suggestions in later revisions.

Step Five: Revising a Script

Storyboarding required students to examine their scripts closely. All needed some degree of rewriting and "reseeing." I set up revision stations around the classroom to provide prompts and writing exercises designed to assist in revision. As Heard explains, revision "involves changing the meaning, content, structure or style of a piece of writing rather than the more surface changes that editing demands" (2003, p. 1). To that end, students' work centered on bringing voice to their pieces or on helping the events come alive for the viewer-reader. Each student completed at least two revision exercises, providing different entrances into their writing and more fuel for our daily conferences.

Option 1: Highlighting
Students marked up their scripts, highlighting all of the action in

green and all of the reflection in pink. Too much pink indicated too much preaching. Too much green indicated that the writer was telling an anecdote with no implications.

Option 2: Timeline
Students rearranged the order of events, making them either more or less chronological (Heard 2003, p. 99).

Option 3: Exploding Sentences
There are two possible plans of attack here. First, writers could work to explode the sentence into a slow-motion retelling (helpful to the text that will be read aloud). Or, writers could think of the explosion as more of a magnifying glass, focusing in on pin-pointed, targeted specifics (Heard 2003, pp. 32–38).

The last stage is for students to transfer their script to a readable form as most of these strategies lead drafts to be written on, crossed out, and packed with marginal notes. Students are shocked when I hand out 4×6 cards and insist that the script be no longer than the front of the card. Again, we're aiming for precision within an end product that should not screen for any longer than two to three minutes. The 4×6 card helps students to focus, to weed out phrases that don't take the reader anywhere, and to home in on the question and eventual payoff.

INTO THE COMPUTER LAB

The Tools
In order to build their digital stories, students needed to import or digitize their photos, add transitions and special effects to how they played, record narration, add a soundtrack, and burn their finished work to a CD. Students had limited time using the classroom computers but were able to come in after or before school, use computers in the media center, or work from home or the community library. Because several students had better tools at home, they built from home, bringing in work to meet my "checkpoints" on their progress.

Again, we worked with iMovie and Windows MovieMaker as our primary tools. Some students elected to work with Adobe Premiere, much higher-end software with both a high threshold and a high ceiling. All of those students had prior exposure to working with Premiere in a digital art course offered during the same semester. This project could, again, be completed using multimedia software such as PowerPoint, but the filmic nature of the final products generated using the digital video editing software provided both a hook and a polished end-product. It led students to voice their confidence in working as both writers and readers in developing compelling visual, textual stories.

Central to the construction was a rule that emphasized content over presentation, setting the balance at 80 percent content and 20 percent effect. Without the rule, students were caught up in zooms, pans, and special effects that showed knowledge of the tool but little control of the story. By putting the story first, students were selective about effects, choosing those that drove the story farther as opposed to those that mimicked what might be seen in films or television. I continually found myself reminding students that one of the essential elements of digital storytelling is economy.

When the Technology Fails and Other Lessons Learned . . .

The downside of working with technology in classroom instruction is its lack of dependability. Digital video tools such as iMovie and Windows MovieMaker are new and still a bit "glitchy." As we worked through the last two days of the project, we were plagued with crashing machines and temperamental equipment. (Students insisted the problems must have been the result of the hamsters inside of our CPU's taking a break instead of running on their wheels to provide power.) The good news is that even in the short amount of time since we completed this project, each of the software programs has developed substantial free updates, and our school server got a little more robust. Some hints and tips to help you along the way:

1. **Save early. Save often.**

   Construction of the story when working with digital video tools like iMovie or MovieMaker can move rapidly. Given that, students (and teachers) need to be reminded to continually save their work, especially as earlier versions of the software (which are most prevalent in our schools) tend to be less stable. All it takes is a locked computer at the close of the class period for a student to fall significantly behind. Students were often amused by my calls to save their work. I quite literally kept an egg timer ticking throughout the period, in an attempt to remind students to save every four minutes.

This isn't a golden rule in terms of the time allocated, but it is essential that students save each time they make some significant changes to their work. Then, in the event of a crash, they have something to return to.

2. **Follow the specific order of the steps—write, plan, discuss, sequence images, add narration, adjust timing, add effects/ transitions, and add soundtrack.**
If students are instructed to follow the specific sequence of steps, there are two central advantages. One, teachers can easily track individual progress using a chart placed on a blackboard or classroom whiteboard. Second, students will maximize instructional and lab time when the tasks are well-framed and specific. The order is designed to tap into the organic process of storytelling as well as to work with some of the "quirks" that exist in different digital video tools.

3. **Require "entrance tickets" before entering the computer lab.**
Those classrooms where students complete script drafts and storyboards apart from computers have been more efficient and have yielded more powerful, more focused student stories. The script and storyboard provide students with a space in which to pre-plan how images will appear on the screen, and encourage precision, allowing images to speak and ultimately do heavier narrative work. Students who haven't had these steps completed before sitting down at a computer regularly lose significant amounts of lab time as they lack a focused plan or even materials to reference.

4. **Maintain backup copies of student work.**
This is another "best practice" when working with any technology. Never save in one place when you can save in two. File sizes of digital videos, even those that are close to two minutes in length, can get large. I asked students to save their files to CD's as well as their school network folders. That way, each could work from any machine and there was a backup copy in case a file did not want to open or be read.

5. **Narrate in small "chunks."**
Recording narration sentence by sentence allows students maximum control over the pacing of their work. Files are simpler to manage.

Inevitably, students who choose to record the script as one large file end up regularly re-recording as it only takes one mispronounced or even deleted word to require beginning again.

6. **Focus on the writing/reading elements of the project.**
This project is full with the practice of what good readers and writers do in working with and crafting print text. To that end, when glitches occur, instead of seeing them as time lost, focus on the time gained as an opportunity to further refine and develop the script and/or storyboard. Don't let the technology get in the way of the story.

7. **Copyright matters.**
Students regularly want to use images gathered from online sources or music downloaded from online repositories. Where this immediately puts materials into students' hands, teachers absolutely must emphasize the need to work within copyright law. I require that students and teachers use their own original images and royalty-free soundtracks. Raising the subject requires that you spend time teaching about what is and is not legal to use.

Screening, Viewing and Discussing . . .

At the close of our work, we screened the finished products, complete with popcorn and student-written feedback. Shared responses celebrated students' attempts to reflectively add meaning to past events and often requested more detail. Others explored technical suggestions for both the presentation and the content, using cinematic terms or referring to texts that we had read. These early conversations marked the start of a collaborative interpretive community that was a safe, supportive structure for their talk and interaction as readers and as writers.

Ending Points

Kylene Beers writes in *When Kids Can't Read* that she "wants to teach kids how to struggle successfully with a text" (2002, p. 16). I firmly believe that engaging readers is my critical teaching responsibility. While I was working here to lead students to really struggle with published personal narratives, my goals were much bigger. As students were not satisfied with only reading someone else's words or experiences, I wanted students to struggle with their words and experiences, to work as writers and readers, and to reinvent their understanding of how they functioned within that role. I wanted them to tap into robust communication tools to tell their story verbally, visually, and powerfully. By allowing each student to see that "all ways of seeing have their silences and their exuberances" (Myers 1996, p. 134), I hoped to create a starting point from which they would see value in their work as scholars.

As with all terms and instructional strategies, there has been "term drift" when it comes to what digital storytelling entails. To some, it's using PowerPoint to create a multimedia, five-paragraph essay. To others, it's using iMovie to capture class events like a Mock Trial or a symposium of student presentations. In my classroom, I've "reinvented" the model to include "digital memory boxes" (collections of readers' artifacts gathered while reading a class novel) or visual literacy narratives (see Chapter 3). Whatever reinvention we use, there are some essential elements that my students argue must be in place: **images, narration/voice,** and **motion.** Some tools allow the product to be filmic, and others, like PowerPoint, lead to a slide show product. Again, we aren't concerned about the tools used but the process and understanding gained. Elliot wrote in his journal that "what makes this different is that it's somewhere between a movie and a slideshow but that it allows my thoughts and voice to be on the screen with the images that I see in my head."

At the end of our first "go" at using digital storytelling in the classroom, more students had completed the project than any other assignment we'd undertaken thus far. More important (and more important than the data that the school system hungered for), students were listening, reading, writing, and seeing the class in a different way. I won't say that they were all engaged and raring to go, but Rochelle, who previously did little more than inhabit her seat in class, was writing more regularly and eager to jump into class discussion of the texts that we read. Sahar and Joscisa came into class talking about English class. And the annotated list of "read books" that Elliott kept in the front of his class journal began to grow. For us, this project was a very real starting point.

ONLINE RESOURCES

Center for Digital Storytelling
www.storycenter.org

BBC Digital Storytelling Project
www.bbc.co.uk/wales/capturewales/

PBS—Telling a Story
www.pbs.org/civilwar/cwimages/tellingStory/flash.html

3: Meeting a Reader: A Literacy Narrative

Pacey was the first student to take me up on the challenge of developing a visual literacy narrative. He was enrolled in the film studies program at our high school, which provided an instant "hook" into this assignment. What started as a script written on a single sheet of notebook paper grew into a five-minute narrative of his experiences as a reader.

In the early days of class, I'd come to know Pacey as a well-liked student with a great sense of humor—but one who did just enough work (written, performative, participatory) not to show up on my radar screen. However, through his literacy narrative, I came to know Pacey as a non-reader and non-writer.

His story began with images of Pacey as a toddler, snuggled into his parents' laps with *Goodnight Moon* and other "standards." I expected to begin by hearing about his early literacy experiences, and yet, his voice-over launched right into where he was as a reader today. He spoke of English class as "the place that kills your reading, teaching you to read to not fail" and of reading as a lonely activity. Here, alongside idyllic images of Pacey as a child reader were the words of "Pacey the school reader, a role I play because you require it from me."

Simply put, I learned more about Pacey in those five minutes than I ever thought possible.

Big Ideas: Our Reader's Stories

As the first assignment in my high school English classes, regardless of grade level or ability descriptors, I asked students to compose a letter, introducing themselves to me as a reader. The lesson began with a discussion of a range of suggested reading lists that I'd pulled from Quindlen's *How Reading Changed My Life* (1998) and Burke's *I Hear America Reading* (1997). I'd talk at some length about my own experiences as a reader, holding up my father's bedraggled, yellowed copy of *Moby Dick* that took us several years to read aloud or my beloved copy of *Ballet Shoes,* complete with duct-taped edges that no longer held the binding together. We'd discuss several of the letters that Jim Burke's class had received from across the country, ranging from students in kindergarten to a convict serving a life sentence. Over the years, our texts grew to include the 1999 *MLA Top 100 Books of the 20th century,* examined alongside Steve Martin's parody that ran in the *New Yorker.* I'd ask students to take a risk and share their own stories about reading.

The letters that students wrote were honest, surprising, and set the tone for much of our work ahead. In some classes, a surprising number of my students spoke of being defeated by grades, reading groups, and pull-outs. For them, reading was neither purposive nor pleasurable. Those books that left impressions were the novels that they'd failed to understand in class, and which continued to resurface in summer school or later grade levels of study. Students were frank about their strategies, explaining what it meant to fake their way through in-class reading, paying attention in class to what the teachers or "smart kids" said about texts in order to know what would be needed on a test. Meaning wasn't theirs. Some could decode but not understand. Others simply weren't willing to even open the book.

For other students, reading was an immersive and necessary experience. They spoke of "literature as a life manual" or of the excitement they experienced in being moved by story. I strongly remember JaNhea's narrative as she explained her experiences in refining a shower-reading technique, requiring that she use one hand to hold the book, and the other to "squeegee shampoo up her neck and onto her head, just because she didn't want to waste the time away from what she wanted to read." Maybe it was the classes that I was assigned to work with, or maybe it was the culture of our school which tended to focus on reading as an assignment or reading as homework rather than reading as fun, but I found that I had far fewer of these kinds of letters.

Instead of asking for a letter, I opened the assignment differently, asking students to compose a literacy narrative—their story as a reader and writer up until the current moment in which we are meeting in English class. Literacy narratives invite students' own stories and experiences into the classroom, providing a writing space meant for the exploration of what student writers think, read, understand, and know about their own skills and experiences. Myers explains that "reading and writing are acts of self definition," and the literacy narrative is a space for students to explore those selves (Myers 1996, p. 130).

INTO THE CLASSROOM: WRITING A VISUAL LITERACY NARRATIVE

Digging Deep

Writing allows us to explore, challenge, and ultimately act on what we know, but we first have to discover what it is that we have to say. I wanted students to work beyond what could be a surface-level piece, something that dashed over what they'd read—or not read—and referred to the course as a place for that to be fed or be changed. For this task, we started with a simple prompt—asking students to bring two "reading artifacts" to class before I had introduced the assignment or had them put pen to paper. Some students brought worn copies of children's books, and others brought artifacts that pointed to where they did their best reading—blankets, some flashlights, and, in one case, a bottle of shampoo (the label of which had been the text the student was most likely to read on any given day).

Pacey brought in a piece of finish line from his cross country meet the previous day. He explained in his reflective writing that:

So, to me, reading is something that I get through so I can cross the finish line. No hidden mysteries there. I read to get it done. I get it done so I can move on to what I really want to do. Enough said.

Students were also asked to make an annotated bibliography of the books found in their home, on their bookshelves, or in the place where they most often read. This opened Pacey some, as he began to write about the library media center. These words became a base for a large section of his eventual narrative:

I don't hang out in libraries. I stopped in the media center because it was the one place that wasn't littered with kids that I didn't know and who didn't seem at all interested in the Navy brat who had just stumbled through the door. The librarian, Mrs. Shina, noticed me, called me over and handed me a card. I didn't know what to

> *say or think. She thought I was a reader. The card had my name on*
> *it, and there was something oddly attractive about how the plastic*
> *cover caught the light. She handed me a book and nodded*
> *toward the couch in the corner, away from the window.*
> *It was as if she knew.*

He then listed the books that he'd read with her—*Ender's Game, Holes in My Life, Eragon,* and *Milkweed.* His annotations didn't focus on the story in the novels, but on the dates he began and finished each title, and the places on the shelves where she'd kept the book for him to collect and read.

In an attempt to push students further, we also did a lot of what I called "reading to write." Here, I pulled out several letters from Burke's *I Hear America Reading* (1997), along with editorials written in response to the 2004 "Reading at Risk" NEH Study. It was important to me that they see how other readers responded to what it meant to read, and that our discussions of these texts trigger thoughts for students that might not have otherwise surfaced.

Making Meaning (on Paper and on the Screen)

Once we'd spent time discussing reading, a reader's work, favorite texts to re-read, and those books that my students referred to as "taught to death," we moved on to writing their narrative scripts. Alongside this writing, similar to what we do with digital storytelling, students created storyboards to help guide the visual writing that needed to be done in anticipation of pulling together a "filmic" narrative. Most students planned to take pictures of their reading places (however "untraditional" it seemed to include a bench at the bus depot or the breakroom at the 7–11 as a reading place) or the people who had influenced their habits (good and bad). Others planned to use more abstract images, scanning original work or relying on a class CD of images from the holdings of the National Gallery of Art in Washington, D.C.

For Pacey, it wasn't enough to use pictures to show the places or texts that had influenced his path as a reader. Instead, he wanted to take a bigger risk and reveal more of what he knew and experienced. He explained in his writer's journal:

> *I need to be able to show you what I do when I read. For Alyssa, this*
> *meant showing her comfy chair and favorite throw. For me, I think*
> *it means showing with a video camera how I work around a page.*

It might be hard to get it right, but I think that is the only way that someone can read this narrative and know anything about who I am as a reader.

Pacey used one of our class digital cameras to record short clips of his paths through the first few pages of *Holes in My Life,* the first book he'd read with Mrs. Shina. Instead of working left to right, he wove in and out, and up and down the page, using Adobe Premiere to add color and pull viewer's attention to the lines as he worked to connect, reread, gloss, reread, and construct meaning.

This wasn't an assignment that I wanted to command too much instructional time. Because only fourteen students of the twenty-eight in this class chose to create a visual narrative, I was able to cycle them through the three computers in the classroom, and provide time before and after school for them to develop their pieces. Further, they also composed outside of class, at home, and in film classes that the school offered. However, if I were working with a full class of visual literacy narratives, I'd set the same kinds of time limits that are described in Chapter 2. Without parameters, these are the kinds of technology-infused activities that can become unwieldy and devour instructional time.

Shaping the Story

Revision is typically a tough task for student writers, and revision in this activity was not an exception to that rule. In this case, a great deal of that resistance came from the idea that students didn't feel it necessary to take a second chance at developing their own written version of their experiences. What opened students in this case was a series of questions taken from Katherine Bomer's *Writing a Life:*

1. Where are you in this piece?

2. Revise by telling the truth. (about how you felt)

3. Revise by telling "lies." (or, compensate for what you can't remember)

4. Revise by leaving things out.

5. Revise by telling another side of the story (2005, pp. 159–168).

Bomer's questions made revision accessible, and encouraged students to take on sections of their writing, as opposed to reworking the entire narrative.

In Pacey's case, he focused on what he could leave out. The difficulty he began to face when putting the images with his recorded narration was that there were too many words that were telling his readers what to see, what to think, and so on. In his revision, he cut description, offering:

I've never seen a movie or a documentary that had someone talking the whole way through like this. Yeah, it's my story, but it's going to become my story as seen by a reader. Why give it all to them? I want them to work.

Pacey's written script went from the front and back of a sheet of college-ruled notebook paper, to only the front of one page. It wasn't that the length was an issue; it was that he needed to provide space for the images to take on some of the narrative work (Figure 3.1).

FIGURE 3.1: A SECTION OF THE TIMELINE FROM PACEY'S VISUAL READER'S NARRATIVE

"Talking the Text"

We took time in class to view or read-aloud those literacy narratives that students wanted to share. For one of the first times in my teaching, I had unanimous participation. As Sahar explained, "Well, that's just because we all want to talk the texts . . . We got to hear the other reader's stories, and now we need some airtime, too." We hadn't conducted a formal peer review, and, for many of the students, this was a read-aloud in order to see how another reader made meaning from their experiences.

Students were invited to use time before or after their reading or screening to reflect on their process of developing the narrative or to share something that would help to focus the audience's attention on a particular aspect of the text. Most of the students didn't take me up on that offer, relying on the context of the read-aloud to do the work of setting up what they had to say. Pacey, however, set up his story by offering:

I think that this was the easiest and the hardest writing that I've done. When I work on a film, it's external. This is internal. It's a little raw. I'm going to show you something that I didn't know.

Students were riveted to Pacey's work, which walked them through a place that they knew, only through his eyes. They knew Mrs. Shina. They knew the corner of the library where they'd never noticed him sitting and reading. They knew the risk it took for him to not only admit to the crazy paths that he'd take through the page, but to show it in color, calling attention to its uniqueness, its flaws, and its brilliance. At the end of the film, there was a pause that lasted just long enough for me to grow concerned. And then, they applauded. And Pacey grew before our eyes.

End Points

In starting the school year by recognizing the different reading experiences, talents, and struggles of the students in my classes, I believe that we set a standard for the remainder of the course: that all students were readers. We might not all read the same texts. We might not all read for the same purposes. But, we all engage with words and images and sound in an attempt to make meaning from the texts that we encounter. That's a very big part of what my classes are about. Further, I wanted to establish, from the start of the course, that I valued my students' voices and respected the stories that they brought into the classroom as readers. Yes, we had pressures of state-mandated, high-stakes assessments and a curriculum full of more required content than would be easily understood. But, unless we started by seeing one another and the possibilities of what reading could be, I couldn't see how we were to get to the work at hand.

Pacey wrote, in a final journal entry addressing the project:

I still am not sure that I'd define myself as a reader, but I'm closer. I never sat down and thought about why I read or don't read—it was easier to just not read. Part of me thinks that I was tricked a little into this, but in watching my video, I see myself as reader. It isn't pretty, but it's there in ways that I don't see it if I read through these notes. Not sure what's up with that, but I'm going to keep coming so I can figure it out.

4: Marking a Path through Text

Two weeks into the semester, Dahabo joined my first-period, "on-level" ninth-grade English class, arguably one of the most difficult (and rich) that I'd encountered. The thirty-one students enrolled in the class read and wrote at very different levels, which mirrored the range of their attention levels, curiosity as learners, and investment in the journey ahead. At this stage of the semester, community was dependent upon who showed up, what task we were exploring, and how willing the class was to give it a shot. And Dahabo? She quickly blended into the middle of the third row, quietly observing the class and contributing only when prompted, often leading me to question at the close of a busy day if she'd even been present.

Our first novel was Steinbeck's *Of Mice and Men*, and despite the fact that only one student in the class "fessed-up" to having read an entire novel for any former English class, I built a unit meant to lead students to develop rich, personal responses to the text while also engaging in required film study through the American Film Institute. Students were more than content to view the film but were making minimal progress when it came to engaging with the novel.

With prompting and several in-class models, most students utilized the stacks of sticky notes available in our reading supplies to mark up the text with ideas and questions. We'd use those notes to run hot-seat discussions, enact scenes, construct character journals, and fuel further reading. Momentum built slowly, but as the class became increasingly confident and more engaged in the activities, students were drawn into the print text. And Dahabo? She would physically sit in her group, book in hand, silent. Where students' copies of the novel grew fat with colored notes and active meaning-making, Dahabo's remained slim and closed.

During our weekly scheduled reader's conference, Dahabo explained to me that though she understood the models and instructions offered in class, she "didn't have anything to say" in response to the pages she'd read. The more that I pushed her, the more she revealed, explaining that writing in response to fiction felt awkward because "my words aren't published . . . they can't live in the same space and mean anything."

It turned out that Dahabo's lack of entries had little to do with her comprehension or understanding of the text and everything to do with her lack of confidence in her role and voice as a reader. As I turned the pages of her reader's log, I noticed that most of her responses were graphic, the print text describing the understanding and connections that she depicted through sketches and drawings. She richly described and elaborated on what she had represented, explaining that "I see things in pictures, and I like to write that way."

It was Dahabo's idea to try to use pictures as a means of annotating and marking her way through the novel. Where she saw it as a means of using her visual skills to represent her understanding, I saw it as an opportunity for her to have a presence in the text, working to construct meaning by inserting images and responses onto the page. She identified a series of "logographic cues" which would signal different responses to text (e.g. a chain link fence for an area where she could connect to another text she'd read, or a question mark for those areas which generated confusion). Where she initially drew the images onto sticky notes, she later printed them onto stickers, inserted them graphically when we read electronic text, and even added them to her response journal entries for additional reflection and writing.

We'll investigate the use of logographic cues later in the chapter. What's important here is to recognize how the use of an image allowed Dahabo to enter into a conversation with the print text, build on past knowledge, and develop readings that she felt confident enough to share with other students in the class. My role as teacher wasn't to equip her with a set of canned annotations (the *what* of marking up a text) but to lead her to see *how* to use her understanding to interact with the author's text. We'll follow Dahabo's development, the growth demonstrated by her classmates, and my own learning throughout the chapter.

Big Ideas: Representing Meaning and Transformative Learning

Reading in my classroom is a process of constructing meaning in an attempt to develop understanding and insight. Early in my teaching, this had a great deal to do with asking students to answer multiple-choice exam questions. However, the more I continued to learn and the more interactions I had with the struggling readers who filled my classroom, the more I began to see the importance of asking students to complete tasks that extended their thinking beyond a quick interaction with the text.

I was struck by Anne Berthoff's work with representation, holding that "visualizing, making meaning by means of mental images, is the paradigm of all acts of mind. Students who learn to look and look again are discovering their powers" (Berthoff 1980, 65). The problem was that I had utterly no idea how to translate her words into classroom action. How could I lead students like Dahabo to see as she read and then use that envisioning or "mental movie" to fuel understanding of more sophisticated texts?

Seeing and looking are visual, thus leading me to consider the multiple ways that students could visually construct, represent, probe, and capture knowledge. Several theorists and teacher researchers (Heath 2000, Kress 2003) call for curricula that allow for the construction of images that represent understanding and textual knowledge. Wilhelm even argues that "without a visual model, there will be nothing for students to think with, nothing to think about" (1995, p. 471). The reality was that, in a tight curriculum that clearly laid a path and set very specific activities for my students to complete, there was little support for instructional tasks that my colleagues saw as "simply drawing" or "the easier way to get students to respond to texts."

It was my classroom experiences and the success of some previously struggling students that helped me figure out ways to use what the theorists and researchers suggested while balancing a restrictive curriculum with, more importantly, the individual needs of the students in my classroom. Throughout our work, I began to see a great deal of change not only in how my students participated and engaged in the classroom, but in how they complicated and enriched their work as readers. Students who engaged with the kinds of strategies described throughout this chapter became invested in generating representations and meaning, in communicating that understanding and "seeing" to others, and in returning to the text to verify, explore, and know.

What big ideas did I learn in the classroom and include in the pages that follow? Surprisingly, they weren't ideas about the tools that we used or the texts that we read together. Instead, I realized that developing readers need multiple opportunities to choose, to explore, to test their understanding within literacy communities, and to return to the text to develop their meanings. Learning as readers, as writers, as speakers, and as thinkers happens through discovery, sharing, and dialogue that connects with students' prior experiences and understanding, challenging them to develop new, meaningful insights. Or, as Steph Harvey explains, "with insight, we think more deeply and critically. We question, interpret and evaluate what we read. In this way, reading can change thinking" (Harvey 2000, p. 9).

"DURING READING"

Readers construct meaning as they engage with the words on the page. Effective strategies enacted during this stage of the reading process challenge students to figure out how they are making sense of the text through their active, recursive work as readers. Here, our instructional goals are to:

- evoke/envision the textual world
- make and test predictions
- monitor understanding
- ask questions
- make connections.

Through the kinds of scaffolding in place within these strategies, students enter rich, literary texts, monitor their thinking, bring ideas into discussion, and apply what they read to their own lives.

INTO THE CLASSROOM

Logographic Cues and Graphic Annotation

This strategy requires that students use images to mark up and respond to text in the same ways that

---

WHAT DOES THIS MEAN FOR ME AS A TEACHER?

In developing and executing reading activities in mixed-ability classrooms, my role is one of supporter, facilitator, and perhaps even cheerleader. It's my responsibility to work alongside students and help them name and celebrate their growing skills. Further, it's critical that I model reading strategies and thinking processes for students to help them see how readers make sense of text and to model the complexities of reading as an ongoing thinking process.

we conventionally write marginal notes. Here, we identify and signal meanings with images.

The images on this page are among the twenty cues which Sam, a sixth grader in Ms. Jackson's class, collected and saved for use in marking-up and annotating texts. Images came as he roamed his neighborhood and the school grounds with a digital camera in hand, or were scanned from an album of his former home in Seattle. Students can just as easily draw their logographic cues, as in Dahabo's work described earlier in the chapter.

When working as a reader, Sam pasted these "cues" throughout the text, explaining in his reflective journal that he could "put more meaning into a picture than into notes in the margins."

Previously, the pages of Sam's textbook were blank, containing no annotations, notes, questions, or reactions. In using the logographic cues, Sam lined the pages of *The Giver* with pictures and written notes that extended

FIGURE 4.1: CONNECTIONS

FIGURE 4.2: STOP & THINK. THIS WAS DIFFICULT.

FIGURE 4.3: RICH DESCRIPTION

what he meant to signal through the use of his cues. In other words, Sam constructed meaning through a process of:

- *representation* (selecting the image for the cue),
- *identification/connection* (locating areas in the text and matching them with logographic cues),
- *communication* (placing the image and supplementing with written notes),
- and *interpretation* (making meaning by considering the text, the image, and the notes).

Sam's metaphor was that the cues functioned as road signs, "showing [him] how to work through the words on the pages."

In subsequent work with literary texts in class, Sam continued without prompting to annotate using a combination of consistent logographic cues and marginal notes. These tools provided him with a means to decipher, consider, and interact with the ideas on the printed page. Further, Sam began participating in class book talks and Socratic seminars, now able to draw on direct textual references drawn from his textual notes.

Visual Read-Aloud and the Voices Student Readers Hear

We read aloud in my classroom on a regular basis, whether I'm working with low-level middle school students or twelfth-grade Advanced Placement students. Literature is an invitation to experience, to speak, to have dialogue with others, to question, and to see through eyes that aren't our own. Reading literature aloud allows us not only to immerse ourselves in the story but also to practice, apply, and later reflect on specific reading strategies. Engaged reading is a visual experience, evoking the creation of an imagined story world often referred to as a "mental movie." Not only do student readers need to learn to develop these "mental movies" from the words on the page, but they absolutely must explain, connect, and reflect upon their own understanding via their own storytelling, a process of constructing and communicating meaning for others.

The Visual Read-Aloud

In creating a visual read-aloud, students read print text, generate visual representations of the envisioned story world, and use a multimedia presentation or digital video software to fuse the visual with a recorded narration of the text. Here, the technology allows for a film-like product that replicates both the visual and oral components of the "mental movie."

Allington is quick to point out that reading aloud is still one voice reading aloud, arguing that "when children read aloud, only one child is necessarily reading although other children might be following along or reading ahead" (Allington 2000, p. 33). What makes this project different from round robin reading paired with a picture is that the reading is conducted and narrated by each student, represented through multiple and varying depictions, and analyzed and discussed by the entire class community.

Within the visual read-aloud, we build from Langer's notion of "envisionment" in that student representations of the story world are "dynamic sets of related ideas, images, questions, disagreements, anticipations, arguments, and hunches that fill the mind during reading, writing, speaking or other experiences where one gains, expresses, and shares thoughts and understandings" (Langer 1995, p. 9). For Dahabo, this presented a new obstacle. Where she had gained increased confidence in "discussing" text with the author through annotation and logographic cues, here she needed to exercise a different skill in constructing a tangible representation of what she saw, heard, thought . . . and, ultimately, envisioned.

Dahabo started slowly, working to graphically represent her ideas by drawing, creating collages (using Photoshop Elements or cutting and pasting images together), and painting. She explained in a reader's conference, "now I can't just talk with the book . . . there is more on the line because I have to show what I see." Where some students struggled with their ability to visually represent their ideas, Dahabo was more concerned with the way that she would be positioned in what she created. She explained, "I'm just now figuring out what I want to question and push as I read . . . but pairing my pictures with the words shows where I am as a reader with this book. That's risky."

Dahabo chose *Speak* as her self-selected independent reading novel for the first term of the quarter. In developing her visual read-aloud, she first recorded a selection from the text which, as a reader, she found to be problematic:

> *"You need to visit the mind of a Great One," continues Mr.*
> *Freeman. Papers flutter as the class sighs. The radio sings louder*
> *again. He pushed my pitiful linoleum block aside and gently sets*
> *down an enormous book. "Picasso." He whispers like a priest.*
> *"Picasso. Who saw the truth. Who painted the truth, molded it,*

ripped from the earth with two angry hands." He pauses. "But I'm getting carried away." I nod. "See Picasso," he commands, "I can't do everything for you. You must walk alone to find your soul."

The images that she chose were a combination of the logographic cues she'd used to mark the passage and abstract paintings by Picasso that represented her own confusion about what it meant to see as he did. She explained, "I'm not an artist, but I stopped as soon as I read the last line. I reread this passage so many times, remembering what I knew about Picasso (which was weirdness—not truth), and thinking about how I see." There was also a connection to Melinda, the novel's protagonist. As Dahabo explained, "the eye is my eye but it's also hers . . . what pushes me into and out of this book is that I'm often her—and she's often me."

Dahabo emphasized at the close of her first experience in building the visual read-aloud that she had a difficult time reaching a stopping point. She offered, "it wasn't that I couldn't pick the passage, it was that the more I worked to show, the more I saw . . . Reading kept happening."

Reader's Voice

One surprising element within this work has been students' awareness and expression of the voices that they hear as they read. Some of my student readers who struggle the most lack any voice as their eyes read over the words on the printed page. The narration within the visual read-aloud provides a model that several students have found to "jump start" their own readers' voices.

A more complicated set of voices is heard as students become more proficient and texts become more challenging. Tovani identifies these as the reciting voice and the conversation voice (Tovani 2004, p. 63). The reciting voice simply reads the words from the page while the conversation voice interacts with those same words, questioning, probing, and unpacking throughout the text. It's my students' experience that the reciting voice quickly gives way to the conversation voice once they begin to internalize basic reading strategies.

However, they have a difficult time focusing that voice on the ideas and issues represented within the text. Instead, the voice follows tangents and unrelated topics. Initially, this led Dahabo to stop—completely. Her eyes pulled from the page, the book closed, and her work shifted from developing understanding to trying to get back to where she thought she was supposed to be in the task. She explained, "I don't know how to get back or what it means that I drift . . . and since I close the book, it all stops and goes away . . . even the good stuff."

Interestingly, Dahabo wasn't alone. The visual read-aloud activity opened a space for the class to discuss the voices as we viewed the "finished" products, and Rai, Dahabo, Sam, and others pointed out that there was an important missing component when we included only images and the text read aloud. Rai explained, "I wanted to include the voice I hear as I read this text because it helps and hurts when I'm trying to understand what's happening." When we began to identify those areas where the voices were a distraction, students, including Dahabo, pointed to passages with complex syntax, difficult vocabulary, and changes in voice. They read, reread, and probed those sections in order to discern what was happening. This work eventually built into the visual think-aloud described in Chapter 6 as students wanted to include their thoughts, questions, and challenges within the same text as the visual read-aloud.

Community

Also essential to this work is the notion of community. As Lave and Wenger explain, "learning . . . is a process of becoming a member of a sustained community of practice . . . Developing an identity as a member of the community and becoming knowledgably skillful are part of the same process" (1991, p. 65). The visual think-aloud can be individually or group constructed, but I always anchor the work to either a think-pair-share or some other means of challenging students to share their ideas and products with one another. For meaning making to advance beyond the pairing of images and text, it's important that "individuals consider multiple ways of interpreting and view individual selves within the class community as interwoven" (Langer 1995, p. 4).

The strength of the visual read-aloud is that it allows students to read text aloud, create their envisionment, and fuse the two together in an oral and visual product. We spend significant class time debriefing after viewing each read-aloud, exploring how the print text and the visual work to convey meaning. Here, "students have a concrete reference as they ask themselves and others: Why did you do that? What else can you do?" (Wilhelm 1995, p. 498).

Visual Literature Circle Reports

Literature Circles allow student readers to do the work that proficient, engaged readers do. We read self-selected, interesting books and seek opportunities for rich, authentic discussion. I was surprised to learn how many of my students had engaged in online discussions of what they were reading, ranging from chats about automobile parts to responses within Web logs attached to the *Washington Post* and *New York Times* Web sites. However, these same students were quick to point out that school reading didn't provide them with an opportunity to read anything in which they were invested. Seth, an eleventh-grade student, confessed to me in a literacy narrative that "I don't have to read the stuff for school . . . I just have to talk like the teacher or think like the test." He hadn't read a single assigned novel throughout his high school experience, but was a prolific reader of sports magazines, newspapers, and statistics manuals. In explaining why, he offered that "I don't get the words, and they don't matter to anything I care about."

In a list of the lessons about reading that teachers impart through their classroom practices, Lucy Calkins writes that through our actions or words we often teach students that reading is a waste of English class time; that readers break whole, coherent, literary texts into pieces, to be read and dissected one fragment at a time; and that reading is a serious, painful experience (in Atwell 1998, p. 28). Too often, we ask students to break apart rather than to connect, infer, predict, and converse with the author. Further, we often ask students to do little more than reproduce the text as it appears on the page, "as a kind of getting to grips with what is already there" (Moss 2003, 76). These tasks lead struggling students like Seth to read at the frustration level, defined as working word by word with accuracy levels beneath 95 percent and comprehension below 75 percent of a given text (Betts 1996, p. 46).

Literature Circles crashed miserably in my early attempts as I continued to violate the cardinal rule—let the students choose from an assortment of texts. I felt locked into my nonthematic curriculum and would try to run Literature Circles around *The Scarlett Letter* or *The Great Gatsby* as a means of engaging student interest and generating meaningful discussion. Further, I required students to complete inauthentic, essay assignments at the close of each discussion.

After working with colleagues and attending one of Smokey Daniels's sessions at a National Council of Teachers of English conference, I made some instrumental changes. Instead of remaining locked to a set text, I created thematic units that allowed for student choice of rich, compelling texts that weren't necessarily on the required list but that were rigorous and linked to the themes the required texts pointed toward. My role changed. Instead of sitting in on the Literature Circle, I circled the classroom, listening, observing, and facilitating.

Perhaps the largest change had to do with assessment and the final required products. I now use two varying kinds of culminating reports: "noticings" about group process (Steineke 2001) and products that allow students to advertise or share their understanding and texts with a larger audience. As Daniels writes, "the book projects that follow literature circles are not natural, relevant or energizing activities. Instead, they are something we teachers assign just to evoke a tangible product, something that can be graded" (Daniels 2003, p. 90). I now challenge students to create visual representations of their understanding at various points throughout the evolution of the discussion. These have included:

Book cover redesign

Rashida participated in a group that read coverless, tattered, dog-eared copies of *Holes* contributed to the book room by a local library. Following her work within the group, she elected to represent her understanding by creating a cover that depicted what she saw as the main themes of the book. She explained in a class presentation that "the cover of a book is what draws me to think about what it's really about. I never realized how much it led me to have fixed expectations. Our discussion changed that."

Collages of key characters and/or themes in the text

Paul worked throughout his group's discussion of *Lies My Teacher Told Me: Everything Your American History Textbook Got Wrong* to identify areas of dissonance where his experience and learning conflicted with the content of the book. As a culminating project, he used Photoshop Elements and a collection of images gathered from the Library of Congress's American Memory Collection to develop a collage of themes, big ideas, and responses that he had to the text. He explained, "I wanted to play with historical images in the same way that historians seem to play with (okay . . . interpret) facts. I don't usually get into nonfiction, but this was really different."

KEY INGREDIENTS OF A LITERATURE CIRCLE

Authentic Literature Circles include most of the following ingredients:

*Students **choose** their own reading materials.*

***Small temporary groups** are formed, based on book choice.*

*Different groups read **different books**.*

*Groups meet on a **regular, periodic schedule** to discuss their reading.*

*Kids use written or drawn **notes** to guide reading and discussion.*

***Discussion topics** come from students.*

*Group meetings aim to be open, **natural conversations** about books.*

*The teacher serves as **facilitator**, not a group member or instructor.*

***Evaluation** is by teacher observation or students' self-evaluation.*

*A spirit of **playfulness and fun** pervades the room.*

*When books are finished, **readers share** with their classmates.*

(from Daniels 2003, p. 18.)

Creation of storybooks modeling text structure and bringing in concepts from other content courses

Students within my tenth-grade honors class were challenged to use what they learned from their Literature Circle texts to develop a storybook to be shared with local third graders studying weather. Group B decided to read a collection of Native American myths and modeled the myth structure to create a storybook that fused their understanding of weather events with what they'd learned about Native American storytelling and oral culture. The visual storybook was accompanied by a cassette tape of the students reading the storybook aloud.

Development of a board game based on the plot or issues within the text

Cindy used the inside of a shirt box to develop a board game meant to lead students through the reading of Achebe's *Things Fall Apart.* She offered that "the discussions in my group were the only way I got through this book . . . this game is meant to walk the reader through the same realizations that we made as we read."

ENDING POINTS: DAHABO AND "WHAT READING IS ABOUT"

In late November, Dahabo sat working on a missed assignment as I tore down and began to replace a bulletin board. After watching me quizzically for a few moments, she asked if she could design the next board, sharing an idea for an interactive space where students could all respond to a shared question. She titled it

"What Reading Is About" and presented it to her peers the next day. Comments were added throughout the remainder of the semester and led me to integrate it as a permanent part of the layout of my classroom.

Gallas explains, "to read a text with understanding and insight, we must move inside the text, pulling our life along with us and incorporating the text and our lives into a new understanding of the world" (2003, p. 20). In using the strategies described in the chapter, Dahabo was able to use technology tools to see how a reader can work with text. She was able to experience the construction of her visualized "mental movie." She was able to see those moments when a reader steps in and out of the print text, questioning, analyzing, commenting, and connecting. As she explained, "Reading wasn't just in my head anymore".

While this didn't fill in all the holes in her background or lead to a complete change in her reading behavior or work as a student, it provided her with a successful starting point. She willingly enters class texts, less hesitant and less likely to stop reading at the first sign of trouble. She knows a handful of moves that she can make to understand and then apply what she learns from what she reads. Dahabo *is* a reader.

MANAGING THE TECHNOLOGY

As demonstrated throughout these examples, what's key about our use of technology with these "during reading" strategies is that the technology needs to add instructional value to the task. The technology has to do something better. These same tasks can be effectively accomplished with the use of magazines, scissors, and construction paper. However, the unique capacities of tools like iMovie or PowerPoint allow students to generate short, animated films which more authentically represent the way that they see mental movies and depictions. Yes, these involve a greater investment of time but, in the case of Sam, Toby, and Dahabo, that investment paid off in their increased understanding of how readers work and their self-monitored use of selected comprehension strategies. Most of the use of technology described in this chapter was student-initiated, building from the unique talents and skills that they brought into the classroom. Consider these guiding questions:

What is the value added by using technology this activity?

What are the resources at my disposal?

What do I need to know in order to make this work?

SUGGESTED READING:

Allington, R. 2006. *What Really Matters for Struggling Readers,* 2nd ed. Boston, MA: Pearson.

Beers, K. 2002. *When Kids Can't Read, What Teachers Can Do: A Guide for Teachers 6–12.* Portsmouth, NH: Heinemann.

Harvey, S., and A. Goudvis. 2000. *Strategies that Work.* Portland, ME: Stenhouse.

Keene, E. L., and S. Zimmerman. 1997. *Mosaic of Thought: Teaching Comprehension in a Reader's Workshop.* Portsmouth, NH: Heinemann.

Tovani, C. 2004. *Do I Really have to Teach Reading?* Portland, ME: Stenhouse.

When Adam and I met, he was seated on the floor outside of his third-period class, staring blankly at the book in his hands. The pages hadn't turned in the twenty minutes it had taken me to walk down the hall, retrieve a book from a colleague, drop papers at the media center, and make my way back.

"So, what are you reading?" I asked.

"Nothin' . . ." he started. "Well, this book, but I'm not real into it."

He held up his copy of *The Phantom Tollbooth,* a title I knew well as a reader and as a teacher. I immediately started describing my own enthusiastic experiences in reading the novel as a child, noting the immediate "glaze" that made its way over Adam's eyes.

"Yeah, you're one of them," he interrupted.

"One of who?"

"Word people," he offered.

Not accustomed to the term (and unsure as to whether or not this was a group into which I wanted to be placed), I asked Adam to clue me in.

"Word people . . . Here, let me show you . . . In this book, there is a place called Dictionopolis—you'd remember that because you liked it so much . . . Yeah, so these people have a word market—which is what Mrs. Carter is doing in there now. She's all into it. They've got dictionaries, pieces of paper . . . They're building words, selling words . . . But they miss the big thing—not everybody gets it. I don't get it. I know what I've got to know, but I don't do lists. I don't remember that junk. And if I don't know words, how in the heck am I supposed to do this?"

I bit. I sat down next to Adam and proceeded to have an engaging discussion of the word people, his dislike of English class, and his own frustrations with reading.

He shared, "It's so slow . . . to have to go one word at a time. And when I get stuck on a word, that's it."

During our entire conversation, Adam looked at me distrustingly, as if I were going to rat him out to his English teacher at any given second. Perhaps it was his knowledge that I was, indeed, one of the word people. Perhaps it was that I was asking questions that made him physically squirm (though that could have been the floor we were sitting on). Perhaps it was because he wasn't sure if I was really hearing him.

What I heard was that Adam was a word-to-word, surface reader. His lack of vocabulary and textual confidence, not to mention his lack of strategies, were preventing him from engaging with texts. Further, any attempt at talking about "vocabulary instruction" led him to simply stop talking. For Adam, vocabulary instruction was punitive, something he had to repeatedly endure in an attempt to face what he didn't know. It meant repetition and copying definitions from the dictionary until he gained enough words to move onto a new list.

My goal as an English teacher is to lead students to practice literacy in a way that demands an adequate and expanding vocabulary. I don't doubt that these were Mrs. Carter's intentions as well. However, when students aren't reading regularly, when they don't have strategies for puzzling out unknown words or the equipment upon which to hang new words, they can't begin to enter texts thoughtfully. Instead, they are regularly in the hall, picking at the corners . . .

BIG IDEAS: VOCABULARY STUDY AND READING

My first attempts at teaching vocabulary largely mirrored my learning, resurrecting childhood memories of my father telling me to "go look it up" as I trudged to our family dictionary, muttering the whole way. In my classroom, we began by writing definitions to the weekly list of words, some of which were generated from the books we read, but most of which were set by our vocabulary texts keyed to the state assessments. As you'd expect, the students who knew how to "do school" got fed. Those who didn't? Well . . . they didn't.

I required that students maintain a notebook of new words they discovered while reading throughout the course. Where most students had simple entries, my high-performing readers followed each instruction to the "t," writing the word, its definition, its location, its use in a sentence, and even going so far as to regularly annotate the entry with context and discoveries. In Adam's word journal, I found a list of words, only an occasional definition, and nothing more. Those words that my more challenged readers listed were simpler than I'd expected, and were regularly repeated as I paged through their entries. Further, for those students, these journals were highly private, as if they were a list of their shortcomings as readers as opposed to organic places of discovery and future "power."

It took a year of frustration with those students who weren't gaining ground and my inability to help them to gain even an "adequate" vocabulary for me to start looking outside of my textbooks for answers. I attended sessions, took classes, and struggled against the urge to call back my former students in attempt to plead for a second shot to get it right.

So, what works? And, how much is enough? It's estimated that students learn between 3,000 and 4,000 new words each year, with the typical student knowing some 25,000 words by the end of elementary school and 50,000 words by the completion of high school (Graves and Watts-Taffe 2002). That said, these aren't all words that are directly taught, and the definition of "typical" varies. NAEP reading data demonstrates that the kids who need the most words are seeing the fewest number of words daily. Those in the 90th percentile are reading an average of 40.4 minutes per day, which yields and exposure to 2,357,000 words/year, while those in the 10th percentile are reading an average of 1.6 minutes per day, which yields an exposure to 51,000 words/year. Kids who read beneath grade level need to see a new word approximately forty times to understand and really "own" it (Beers 2003). Those numbers add up to a huge disparity, especially when the predominant instructional model is exactly what was happening in my classroom—distributing a list of "hard" words on Monday, looking up definitions and writing sentences, and testing on Friday.

We know that the most effective methods of introducing new words involve introducing them in groups that share some relationship or characteristic (McKenna 2004). In my classroom work, that meant drawing words out from the required lists and looking to provide context as well as connection. Research also indicates that students need to know the meaning of new words before they encounter them in a piece of text. So, instead of asking students to generate lists of words that were obstacles or new discoveries during reading, I needed to empower them to enter the text informed and genuinely ready to construct meaning as opposed to stumbling their way through, only to revisit the accident site to record what they didn't know.

Where I'd meant for the word journals to provide students with a space for actively participating in their own learning, the research base called for more. Students needed to (1) sense and infer relationships between vocabulary and their own background knowledge, (2) recognize and apply vocabulary words to a variety of contexts, (3) recognize examples and nonexamples, and (4) generate novel contexts for the words we studied (Blachowicz and Fisher 2000). Further, this was as important for out-of-class reading as for those texts and words we explored in class.

More importantly, there was a shift that needed to happen in my understanding of what was important about my students' study of vocabulary. My previous focus was on the breadth of my students' vocabularies (i.e., the number of words for which they could offer a definition) as opposed to the depth and precision of their knowledge when it came to knowing how and when to use those words. Friere and Macedo wrote that "reading does not consist of merely decoding the written word or language; rather, it is preceded by and intertwined with knowledge of the world" (1987, p. 29). That's where we needed to begin—by seeing, valuing, and calling out the knowledge that students brought each day.

INTO THE CLASSROOM

Where the classroom strategies that follow provided students with a visual entrance and often a scaffold into their work with print words, this teaching occurred within classrooms that I would describe as word-rich. "New" words were public and involved my learning and modeling as much as my students' work. What does that mean? I incorporated the words into our discussion and written correspondence. Sure, this meant that there were lots of quizzical looks when I'd toss out that "Jaime looked disgruntled today," but the questions that followed were worth the raised eyebrows. Yes, words hung on the classroom wall and dangled from the ceiling, but we (myself included) also read voraciously. My expectation, regardless of the level of the student, was that students were actively taking in words through as many different forms of text as they found compelling. We talked about the words we read, and we talked about our discoveries. The goal was immersion with a touch of play, and these strategies were a part of both the "hook" and the entrance.

Picturing It: A Series of Vocabulary Activities

Vocabulary Square

This is a paper and pencil activity that is the primary tool in my classroom teaching for working with vocabulary across grade levels and content areas. Developed by Jim Burke (2002), the vocabulary square is a graphic organizer that focuses student attention on a selected word, its roots, its synonyms/antonyms, and its role as a part of speech. Most important to my students' work and understanding was the section of the square that asked them to draw a picture that represented their understanding of the word and its meaning.

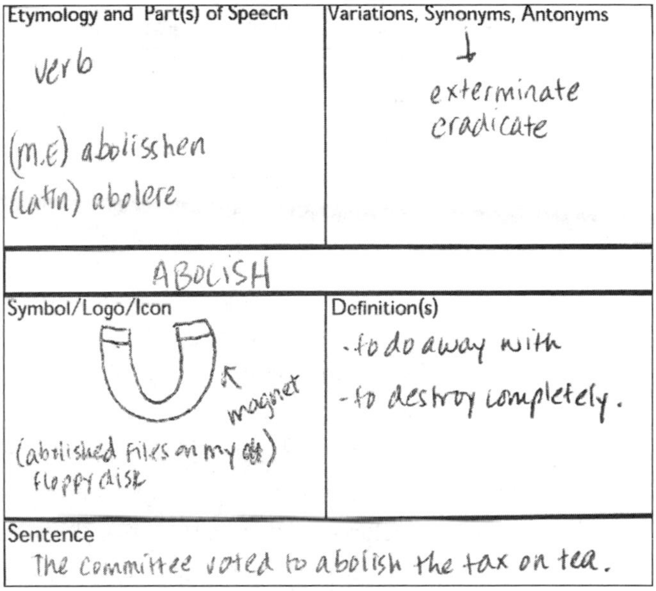

Why is that picture such a big deal? Oftentimes, my students were masters at copying definitions and terms from the dictionary. However, in asking them to create a visual representation of their understanding of the meaning of the term, I was asking students to go beyond "putting the definition in your own words." Instead, I was requiring that they show me the definition through their own eyes.

Some of my students are with me right from the start. They want to convey what they see—and they get right

FIGURE 5.1:
SAHAR'S VOCAB SQUARE FOR "ABOLISH"

Etymology and Part(s) of Speech	Variations, Synonyms, Antonyms
verb (m.e) abolisshen (Latin) abolere	↓ exterminate eradicate

ABOLISH

Symbol/Logo/Icon	Definition(s)
(magnet) (abolished files on my off) floppy disk	· to do away with · to destroy completely.

Sentence
The committee voted to abolish the tax on tea.

to it. For others, there is a great deal of initial "moaning" about having to draw in an English class. We get past it quickly enough once students begin to see the entrance that these pictures provide. As Thomas, an on-level eighth grader, explained, "for one of the first times, I'm actually saying something about what I know, and I don't have to worry about if the words are right. The words, for me, come after the picture. So, I can see what I know, and then write about it."

The vocabulary square is a quick, compact, and tight glimpse into what a student knows about a word—providing me as teacher with a speedy view into what they understand and, perhaps more importantly, what they don't. If I've asked them to define "resilience" and am met with a picture of broken glass, I know that there is a problem. More likely than not, the students' images invite rich classroom discussion about vocabulary—a kind of unprompted dialogue that we never had prior to the use of this tool. Most of my middle and high school English students didn't regularly discuss the differences between the denotation and the connotation of a word's meaning. With these images, it happens readily.

Vocabulary Word Wall (or, The Notebook Made Public)

Once my students became accustomed to depicting their understanding of a word's meaning by drawing it in the vocabulary square, I decided to shake things up a bit. Some students were talented illustrators, but the bulk of my kids usually needed to provide me with some description of what their images were supposed to be. Further, I still had some students who were struggling to convey what they knew graphically or visually. I needed a different tool.

For this task, digital cameras were placed into the hands of students and taken outside of our classroom space. After scrounging what resources I could get my hands on, I ended up with a ratio of about one camera to four or five kids. The challenge was for students to take photos representing the key vocabulary terms studied or, perhaps more importantly, those vocabulary words which students identified as they read. The process (and strength) of the activity was explained by Nada, a fifth grader, offering that "taking pictures lets me understand the definition on my own terms. I picture the word, create the picture, and then start to know the word."

Yes, the camera alone provided motivation. But it wasn't the camera itself as much as it was the process of composing with images. Here, I wasn't just teaching about how writers use words (symbols) to convey their ideas. I was also teaching about how illustrators and photographers create texts and make those texts work. Alongside our discussions of vocabulary were new discussions of how words and images could promote or silence particular views. Students found images to be "everyday," thus making literacy more tangible and valuable to them.

For example, Julia, an eighth grader in Ms. Powell's class, worked to represent "cumulative," "intermittent," and "voice" (see Figures 5.2–5.4).

Students were asked to print several of the images that they collected, using varying sizes of paper to post their work on the rear wall of the classroom. We labeled the posters not with students' names, but with the words defined. The most surprising element of the assignment for me as a teacher wasn't the way that students (even reluctant ones like Adam) took up a camera and actively, mindfully pursued the "right" image. It wasn't the rise in participation and completion of the assignment. It was the "clumps" of students that I found around the back wall three weeks after the first round of the assignment. Students were still talking about the ways the images communicated intended meaning or the ways in which "the picture fit the word."

This wasn't a "one-shot" activity. Instead, it was a task that we repeated as students encountered new reading assignments or we explored new words that they found in independent reading. That said, the more regularly we were acquiring images, the more regularly it became necessary for students to "check out" the cameras as opposed to taking class time for image collection—and we made several "tweaks" along those lines. What stayed

FIGURE 5.2: CUMULATIVE

FIGURE 5.3: INTERMITTENT

FIGURE 5.4: VOICE

constant was the root of the assignment—visually represent the words that you're looking to define.

Beginning with honors-level ninth-grade classes, I also used an extension or reinvention of the activity, challenging students to record literacy events as they experienced them outside of the classroom. In *Changing Our Minds: Negotiating English and Literacy,* Myers explains that speech events are an essential part of situated knowledge, offering students opportunities not only to study language in action but also to examine differences between presentational and conversational modes of communication (1996, p. 143). Extensive discussion in class explores how students use images to capture oral texts and "bring meaning into being" (Kress 2003, p. 70). Building on their visual and verbal literacy skills, my students paired their images with fairly sophisticated written reflections, explaining the event, what meaning it represented, and how it enriched, complicated, or challenged their understanding of literacy. Here, literacy wasn't just limited to the ways in which students engaged with print texts, but instead reached out to include exchanges outside of and beyond the classroom.

Image Flashcards/Visual Word Collection

This is the individualized recasting of the word wall assignment. Here, students use notecards or 4x6 pieces of paper to print out images that they've acquired to represent the definition of a particular word. It's more difficult to manage in that there is never enough technology for each student to have access to a camera at all times—which does result in the occasional student entering the classroom and lamenting that he or she "missed a key shot" the night before. To keep it equitable, I maintain a sign-up sheet, and keep a close eye on which students are dominating that list. Further, with the price-point of cameras bulleting downwards, we're finding that this is the one classroom tool that is in greater supply. Many kids have access at home, and simply bring their saved images on disk, CD, saved to the network, and so on. The key remains the same. Students are using the camera to "read their world" while reading the texts we explore as a part of our class. The image serves as a bridge into doing more than just recalling the definition(s) of the word; it provides students with an opportunity to define, connect, and integrate the word into what is already known.

We've done many different things with the reverse (or blank) side of the card. There is the traditional approach—write the definition (in your own words) along with the part of speech and an example sentence. There is the connect-to-text approach where I ask students to identify and record the use of this word in the texts that we read. Often, I ask students to ask questions that they have about the word, it's use, it's connotation, and so on. This challenges students to confront potentially "problematic" words head-on. Simply put, the value that is added here is that students are using visual images along with a reading/writing space that is portable. These cards are one part study tool, one part reading artifact, and one part "mini-step" into the literacy community within our classroom.

Grouping, Sorting, Labeling

This strategy grew out of lessons that I remember from my own English classroom experiences as a learner. Mrs. Lucas, my eleventh-grade English teacher, regularly typed out (or ran on the mimeograph machine—our "high technology" at the time) the lines of a poem, and then sliced the paper into words or lines that we could "re-assemble" into our own texts. In my classroom, we turned this into a vocabulary lesson, working to sort, categorize, and label words. In each of my sections of English eleven, we again utilized the digital camera to take still shots that represented words, their meanings, their categories, or even their parts of speech. Student teams compiled images in anticipation of the sorting work that we'd complete in class. Again, the use of the visual text here is to support and scaffold student understanding of key vocabulary words, and also to model that the very ways we read images (and the subjects of our images) can help us to engage with print texts.

In working recently with a seventh-grade humanities class in San Antonio, we expanded this activity to include not just the images recorded by the students in the classroom, but also those captured by others across the globe. In anticipation of our study of the Greeks, we used epals.com to communicate with classrooms across the globe (in Maine, Virginia, Kentucky, Texas, Oregon, Florence, London, and Seoul) and asked students to record and send (via email or by posting to a class wiki) images that illustrated our vocabulary words or that demonstrated Greek influences in culture (through architecture, language, art, and so forth). Suddenly, our list had expanded from colonnades and gymnasia to skenes and bouzouki. Here, the technology tools that we used allowed students to collaboratively sort and organize words, expanding their understanding well beyond the definition of the term. The ever-present pressure of the state assessments kept us aware of the "root" list where our study had begun, but students grew to know and understand those ideas much more fully given the immersive, engaging, collaborative lists and groups that emanated from the activity. Sure, it was a fairly high-tech lesson, but one that could just as easily have been conducted between classes in a building or between schools in a community.

What's important in this activity was rooted in the students' use of the words. Yes, we learn new words through repetition and connection to prior knowledge, but the word doesn't become "ours" until we use it. Not only were students creating and sharing visual representations of a word's meaning, but they were actively writing with those words and using them as a springboard into the study of additional words. Their understanding wasn't limited to what a single word meant, but grew to encompass a connected knowledge of words. Perhaps most striking was their unprompted desire to know. Kids who formerly requested the worksheets that they'd been trained to see as "the work of an English class" demonstrated a level of motivation that increased alongside the growing list of words that they saw, understood, and, now, *used*.

Vocabulary Tableaux

I believe in participatory approaches to literacy education. What that means is that my classroom involves reading, writing, moving, expressing, enacting, exploring, debating, visualizing, speaking, listening, and *doing*. This strategy requires, as Asha, a ninth-grade English as a second language ELA student explained, "becoming the words." After selecting the word to be defined, students work either individually or in groups to physically represent and enact its meaning. They create a physical, visual image—which we then record using a camera or video recorder in order to have an artifact that can be used for class study and discussion.

Barry, a self-confessed "non-English kid," became a student who requested that we work on vocabulary tableaux. As a reader, he gravitated toward books he'd already read or studied, what he referred to as "known entities." He lacked confidence to unpack new texts, mostly because of issues with the number of words he saw as roadblocks. I asked him what the draw of the activity was, and he explained:

*Come on, Mrs. Kajder . . . What a no-brainer. When we do that
stuff, I get new shots. Words in the dictionary are shallow. Here,
they go so much further than what Webster says they mean. And,
when I get more words, I get like what I need to get out of reading
what I think I already know. I thought you knew more of that
stuff . . ."*

ENDING POINTS: MORE THAN "JUST WORDS ON A PAGE"

To Adam, vocabulary study was punitive. Instead of opening him to how language works or to an exploration of words rooted in his interests and reading, he followed the traditional set of activities that helped to keep him from the kinds of engaged, rich reading that we, as English teachers, want to see our students experiencing. I have yet to meet an English teacher who entered our profession because he or she really enjoyed looking up Monday's list of new words, copying down definitions, and taking the test on Friday. The strategies in this chapter are meant to set the focus in a different, more generative direction—providing students with opportunities to experience mindful word-play, to visualize, to be motivated to learn new words, and to, ultimately, synthesize, analyze, and interact with words. Ultimately, rich vocabulary understanding unlocks the doors to fluency, and we get there through integration, repetition, and meaningful use (Nagy 1988).

SUGGESTED READING

Allen, J. 1999. *Words, Words, Words.* Portland, ME: Stenhouse.

Allington, R. 2006. *What Really Matters for Struggling Readers,* 2nd ed. Boston, MA: Pearson.

Beck, I., M. McKeown, and L. Kucan. 2002. *Bringing Words to Life: Robust Vocabulary Instruction.* New York: Guilford Press.

Beers, K. 2003. "When Students Struggle with Writing and Reading." Presentation delivered at National Council of Teachers of English National Conference.

6: THE VISUAL THINK-ALOUD

INTRODUCTION: RAI

"Are we reading today?" Rai asked the question as he slumped into our English classroom, dropping his books on a desk with an echoing thud. It was early Tuesday morning and despite several years of teaching experience and question handling, I was dumbstruck. How could that question even exist in an English/Language Arts classroom?

To know Rai is to know what his question was really about. He wasn't kidding. He was asking whether or not he'd have to perform today. Would this class be one in which he needed to put his effort into making it appear that he was completely on task, turning pages, reading and understanding the words on the page when, in reality, he'd be swimming in water well over his head? Rai was a sixth grader reading at a second-grade level, placed into an honors class due to schedule conflicts. As a reader, he had two strategies. The first was to stare at the words while racing through the pages, giving up reading for meaning in exchange for appearing to be on task. The second was simply to stop as soon as he ran into any trouble.

As English/Language Arts teachers, we know Rai and students like him. They are the readers who can read the words, but who cannot say what those words mean once their eyes lift from the screen or paper. They don't see the "mental movie" or hear a reader's voice as their eyes travel the text. They rarely see themselves in the texts provided in school and struggle to see a purpose behind each attempt to find ways in and through what we ask them to read. As Harvey Daniels explains, "the texts we use in our classrooms act neither as mirrors or as windows, challenging students to see themselves in new ways or discover those cultures and communities which are different" (Daniels 2003).

Rai shared in one of our many one-on-one conversations about his work as a reader that he didn't hear an internal reader's voice or visualize the events of the story as he read. He offered, "I struggle through, turning pages, trying to follow the words and ignore silence." His honesty pushed me to revisit professional journals, books, materials from workshops, and the texts of former lessons and lesson plans, looking for ways to move him beyond his silence. As I paged through his reader's journal, a starting place began to take shape. Driven and engaged by the visual, Rai excelled at activities like story mapping or graphic notes, tasks which challenged him to construct and represent his developing understanding. I saw these as beginnings, moments when he was beginning the steps needed to construct a "mental movie."

Slowly, I began to reconstruct a reading strategy centered on reinventing a familiar best practice, think-aloud, and using the few technologies available in the classroom space to make the process visual, auditory, and rich with reader's thoughts, ideas, and understanding. Here, technology was used to further instructional goals, not because the tools were available or even current. As Leu notes, "technologies potentially alter how we teach, the way we learn, and what we learn about" (2002, p. 743), and here they allowed us to merge the visual with the oral in one textual space. The approach hooked students, allowing them to engage in rigorous comprehension work, and to produce a technically sophisticated product in terms of the skills and strategies they applied as readers, not just as users of a specific technology tool.

BIG IDEAS: THINKING ALOUD

Think-Aloud as a Comprehension Strategy

Think-aloud is a research-based best practice in reading instruction. Here, readers work to read print text aloud, pausing at various intervals to insert their own comments and reflections. In other words, "think aloud involves making one's thoughts audible and, usually, public—saying what you are thinking while you are performing a task, in this case, reading" (Duke and Pearson 2002, p. 214). The strategy makes the mostly invisible process of readers and writers open and tangible. Think-alouds are usually either oral or print texts, challenging the reader to record his or her responses, thoughts, questions, and ideas next to the text segments that are addressed.

Expert readers use the think-aloud as a space for inference, connection, and elaboration, where novice readers use it as a place to connect details and develop a literal reading. Think-alouds create a space for modeling what readers do, demonstrating how readers talk about applying strategies by stopping and saying, "This is a point where I ought to visualize the scene depicted" or questioning "What can I do to keep all of this information straight?" Here, comprehension is about "understanding and connecting as opposed to what happens if students' pronunciation is correct" (Allington 2001, p. 96).

What Is a Visual Think-Aloud?

The act of reading is the "reader's evocation of the text as imagined, visualized, and experienced" (Wilhelm 1995, p. 120). Engaged reading is a visual experience, evoking an imagined story world. Dyson takes this further, offering that the "images and the rhythm are the literary equipment which form the story" (Dyson and Genishi 1994, p. 4). Not only do student readers need to learn to develop these "mental movies" from the words on the page, but they absolutely must explain, connect, and reflect upon their own understanding through their own storytelling, a process of constructing and communicating meaning for others.

In Rai's class, we worked to reinvent the think-aloud, fusing the oral or print work done by the the reader within the text with the visual imagery elicited by the story world. Using digital images, scanners, and a digital video software tool such as iMovie or presentation software such as PowerPoint, students worked to create a visual think-aloud, a short digital movie which included both a visual representation of their constructed story world and narrated audio tracks offering their think-aloud. Not quite film and offering more than a slideshow, students identified the products as "class movies of what reading looks like."

For the visual component of the work, students took original pictures using the digital cameras, scanned photos from existing albums brought into the classroom, scanned original art or worked with art already digitized on a class set of CD's from the National Gallery of Art or available at the Museum of Modern Art's Web site. Original photographs featured items from home, familiar scenes, or even images taken on the school grounds. Again, the images were selected or created on the basis of their ability to represent segments of the student's envisioned story worlds. These were aligned in the image line of the timeline in iMovie or were placed on slides in PowerPoint. If using iMovie, the verbal component of the work used one line of the audio track for recording a read-aloud of selected text (i.e., the middle lines in Figure 6.1). The second was used for inserting their think-aloud comments (i.e., the bottom lines in Figure 6.1). If students used PowerPoint, they needed to record their read-aloud and think-aloud comments in one long take, as opposed to the advantage of the dual audio track within iMovie. In other words, the product fused a read-aloud (see Chapter 4) with a think-aloud, using images to represent the reader's envisionment and using audio to communicate textual understanding, connections, and insight.

FIGURE 6.1: iMovie Timeline

INTO THE CLASSROOM

Timeline for the Week (and Work) Ahead

In order to complete this project, students needed to develop the think-aloud and learn about the technology tools (i.e., iMovie or PowerPoint) which allowed them to construct and produce their work. Always a planner, I found it helpful to outline (see Table 6.1) our path for the instructional week, again to ensure that the focus was on developing student readers' skills, not on teaching technology tools.

TABLE 6.1: Timeline of Instructional Events

CATEGORY OF ACTIVITY	STRATEGY	INSTRUCTIONAL TIME
Prereading	Teacher models think-aloud strategy to read introduction to a self-selected novel	Day One (~20–30 minutes)
Prereading	Class discussion of reading strategies and what a reader does	Day One (~20 minutes)
During Reading	Begin reflective reading log/journal	Day One homework.
During Reading	Sparks collection	Day Two (~45 minutes)
During Reading	Evaluate questions (using Harvey's thick/thin criteria)	Day Two (~10 minutes)
During Reading	Think-pair-share discussions	Day Three (~55 minutes)
During Reading	Storyboard and gather/create images	Day Three (and homework ~10 minutes)
During Reading	Script writing	Day Four (~40 minutes)
Construction	Arrange and sequence images	Day Four/Day Five (~10 minutes)
Construction	Record narration	Day Five (~90 minutes available)
Construction	Special effects, transitions, "catch up"	Day Six (~90 minutes available)
Culmination	Screening and discussion	Day Six/Seven (~90 minutes available)

Description of Tasks

Prereading Assignments

Day One

Our work was anchored within the second independent reading unit of the semester, inviting and challenging students to select a text that evoked their interest and led them to "stretch" their skills as readers. For resources, students were provided with annotated bibliographies of those books available in the class library as well as several "book talks" offered by students who were selected at random from a hat. Students also had the option of bringing a book from home as long as it met with the classroom teachers' approval. Once the books were selected from the class library and texts brought from home were approved, students were asked to select the first ten pages or first chapter as the content for the think-aloud.

Because this was our first "go" at working with think-alouds, I started this first class with a teacher-directed read-aloud, a model for the types of thinking and work that could be conducted within students' virtual think-alouds. I modeled the selection process and early think-aloud, providing time for class discussion and debriefing after the think-aloud was conducted. Because students were familiar with the read-aloud as a strategy, most of our discussion centered on the types of questions that a reader might ask of a text or, for those students who weren't quite with me, the "number" of times that I'd be looking for students to break into a dialogue with the text.

Rai's Selected Text

Though the class had read Lois Lowry's *The Giver* two months before, this was the novel Rai wanted to explore in his think-aloud. He had missed several days of the unit and had not read past the first five pages of the novel, explaining that he "just didn't get it." *The Giver* is a challenging fantasy novel which depicts a utopic vision of a colorless, black-and-white community built on the principles of "sameness," sacrifice, and lack of individual choice. In our unit, we'd started with a community-building naming ceremony, discussed the choices and rules in place in students' lives, generated a class list of qualities of an "ideal community," and produced a lively "Pro-Sameness/Pro-Diversity" debate. Rai was absent for most of these activities, skipping first period English because of his inability to engage with and read the novel. Where I had worked to support him with several acceleration activities prior to the class's work with the novel and scaffolding meant to help him into and through the reading, the simple reality was that there was only so far that we could go when he appeared less and less often.

Rai selected to read *The Giver* for two main reasons: to try to work through a novel that his peers greatly enjoyed and to be able to complete a class novel for the first time. Where part of his confidence in selecting a challenging text came from our conversations and his sense of increased support, much of it also came from the class discussion that revealed several students' perceptions about what reading required and involved. He explained, "We were all trippin' up on the same ideas. I don't feel like I'm the only one, and I also don't feel pressured. Instead, we're trying something new to see if it works."

Day Two

Equipped with sticky notes or pads of paper, students read the first five to ten pages of their selected text, noting what we referred to as "sparks"—areas where they could connect another book or a prior experience, questions they had as they read, observations they made about the writer's style, predictions, evaluation comments, or "aha" moments. Rai wrote in his journal about his surprise at this process, explaining, "I've never talked in a book before. I thought it was a one-way thing, not something where I could ask. Yes, we've been told that real readers do this—but this is my first time. I hope that I did this right."

The next stage of the activity started with a "think-pair-share" where students synthesized and summarized aspects of their reading experience. Students self-selected their partners, most choosing friends who read at about the same pace or level. Rai explained, "I chose my partner by thinking about who would be the most open to my ideas and who would understand that I'm not real good."

Next, students were instructed to follow two additional higher-order tasks. In reading and responding to the next two pages of their texts, students were to follow the same response steps in generating their "sparks," adding periodic inference statements by following the formula "It says . . . I say . . ." (Beers 2002). The final step was to evaluate the questions they generated according to Harvey's criteria for thick vs. thin questions (Harvey & Goudvis 2000).

Rai's "sparks" in just the first few pages of reading provided a clear glimpse into his thinking and revealed his attempts toward understanding terms, activating prior knowledge, and making inferences when it came to piecing together multiple sections of text as the story unfolds. The following table offers several of the "sparks" that he wrote in response to reading a few pages into Chapter 1. The text in the column to the left is Lowry's original work. The center column offers Rai's "sparks," edited only for spelling. His comments fit into one of the following categories of response that I had described and discussed with the class: connecting to prior knowledge, summary, reactions to the text, questioning the text, connecting to characters, and self-monitoring. Later in the class work, Rai identified the comment types as listed in the third column.

TABLE 6.2: RAI'S INITIAL "SPARKS"

OPENING TEXT FROM CHAPTER 1	RAI'S "SPARKS"	COMMENT TYPE
He had been frightened then. The sense of his own community silent, waiting, had made his stomach churn. He had trembled.	Why start a novel with fear? Who is speaking—and how does he know so much?	Questioning the text Questioning the text
But it had been nothing. Within minutes the speakers had crackled again, and the voice, reassuring now and less urgent, had explained that a Pilot-in-Training had misread his navigational instructions and made a wrong turn. Desperately the Pilot had been trying to make his way back before his error was noticed.	So, a pilot made a wrong turn. I don't get why this is important.	Questioning the text
NEEDLESS TO SAY, HE WILL BE RELEASED, the voice had said, followed by silence.	What does it mean to be released? Is he in jail? Who talks like this?	Questioning the text
There was an ironic tone to that final message, as if the Speaker found it amusing; and Jonas had smiled a little, though he knew what a grim statement it had been. For a contributing citizen to be released from the community was a final decision, a terrible punishment, an overwhelming statement of failure.	I'm confused. It's grim but funny? How are you released from the community—and how could that be funny? Who is this speaker?	Connecting to prior knowledge

TABLE 6.2: RAI'S INITIAL "SPARKS" [CONT.]

OPENING TEXT FROM CHAPTER 1	RAI'S "SPARKS"	COMMENT TYPE
Even the children were scolded if they used the term lightly at play, jeering at a teammate who missed a catch or stumbled in a race. Jonas had done it once, had shouted at his best friend, "That's it, Asher! You're released!" when Asher's clumsy error had lost a match for his team. He had been taken aside for a brief and serious talk by the coach, had hung his head with guilt and embarrassment, and apologized to Asher after the game.	This is like how we can get into trouble for saying "I'm going to shoot you" or "I'm going to kill you" within school. This releasing must be a pretty big deal.	Connecting to prior knowledge
Now, thinking about the feeling of fear as he pedaled home along the river path, he remembered that moment of palpable, stomach-sinking terror when the aircraft had streaked above. It was not what he was feeling now with December approaching. He searched for the right word to describe his own feeling.	This is mixed up (but I know what it's like to see planes where they shouldn't be and be afraid of that). Before, he was scared. Now he's unsure? Why does it matter if it's December? I must have missed something.	Summary Self-monitoring
Jonas was careful about language. Not like his friend, Asher, who talked too fast and mixed things up, scrambling words and phrases until they were barely recognizable and often very funny.	Words seem to be a really big deal in this book. I just reread this whole first part in order to make sure I didn't miss any words or big ideas.	Self-monitoring

After they had completed their reading, recording, and evaluating, students were then asked to return to their think-pair-share partners in order to conduct a think-aloud, reading two pages of text aloud and inserting their "sparks" as they arose. The classroom came alive. I observed and listened in on students' thinking-aloud to infer, predict, connect, decode, and converse with the author. I was genuinely surprised by the volume of voices that began to fill the classroom space, including Rai's. Kylene Beers explains, "it's more critical for dependent readers to talk about texts during the reading than after it" (Beers 2002, p. 104). With a little bit of scaffolding (teacher-prompted discussion and the think-pair-share reflection), work with the process of generating "sparks" (and what ultimately became a think-aloud) empowered students to be talking about texts before, during, and after their reading. Further, it provided an immediate opportunity to provide guided practice, conference about understanding, and assist with higher order skills. Reading became a process of understanding not just the print text but also the process of encoding it with meaning.

Storyboarding

Day Three

The next stage of the process took the students' think-aloud and asked them to develop a visual component. Students were required to map on paper each image, technique, and element of their envisioned story world by constructing a storyboard. This visual story had two dimensions: chronology (what happens and when) and interaction (how audio information interacts with the images) (Lambert 2002, p. 61). Using a template, students arranged and rearranged images that were listed on sticky notes. In selecting their images, students returned to the text multiple times, as "the choice, representation, and arrangement of images are both a means of making meaning for themselves and of making themselves maximally understood by others" (Mavers 2003, p. 19). Though this was their first experience in storyboarding, students examined two models and quickly proceeded to their own work.

The power of using digital images in this work comes in the students' representations of their constructed story worlds. Maxine Greene argues that "informed engagements with the several arts is the most likely mode of releasing our students' imaginative capacity and giving it play" (2003, p. 125). Several students used this as an opportunity to develop their own artwork where others saw it as an invitation to use pictures of the world around them. Many projected themselves into the textual world by inserting their own image into the photos that they captured or used from online sources. Kress explains that "images are plain with meaning; whereas words wait to be filled" (2003, p. 144). Interestingly, here, words created images that brought students back into closer contact with words. Where many used the digital cameras to capture images that represented the literal or surface-level story world, the exercise became a catalyst for reflection on how to represent more complex responses to how the print text was constructed, what it meant, and how it affected them.

Scriptwriting

End of Day Three/Beginning of Day Four

Conventional digital stories involve the writing of a script that is read aloud and recorded in order to provide narration. The visual think-aloud required scripting of a different sort, challenging students to use their "sparks" to generate the oral think-aloud that they had shared in their peer-teams. Where several students initially began to write out their think-aloud as well, most found it more authentic and responsive to draft the think-aloud as they were recording the read-aloud track. Rai did not write a script, but continued to add to the "sparks" and notes in his text. His think-aloud comments were simply moments where he read what he'd written in the margins or on the sticky notes. He explained, "because I'm rereading again and again, I'm finding new meaning . . . and the script has to allow for that." Here, students self-assessed their own process and understanding as readers while providing me with a direct view into their development.

Design and Production Time

Day Four

All of this initial work took place across three instructional periods, completely apart from the computer. Students needed to complete a storyboard and have a draft of a script (either written or compiled from their textual "sparks") as an "entrance ticket" into the computer lab. They were allowed to choose which software would be used for their think-aloud, with most basing their selection on which tools they knew from either a computer applications course or experience outside our classroom. Only two students in this class had access to computers at home, so the class depended upon experiences in school, the community library, or with friends. Of the twenty-five students in the class, fourteen chose to work with PowerPoint and eleven chose to work with iMovie.

The first task, once students gained access to a computer, was to arrange images in either the iMovie timeline or on slides within PowerPoint. Using the storyboard as a base for this work, students moved quickly to scan, insert, and sequence the images. Rai explained, "This was quick because of all the thinking I'd already done. It was almost annoying because I wanted to move on to the other stuff."

The second stage of construction required students to record their narration either by using multiple audio tracks in iMovie or by recording a single track within PowerPoint. Each computer had a built-in microphone. The most essential component of the scripting and narration process is that it allowed for the student's voice to be present in the reading of the print text. Students were present as readers, writers, and thinkers throughout the project, many for the first time. Though most were initially stuck as they rerecorded initial reading because they were surprised by the sound of their own voice, most became comfortable early into the process, focusing on the meaning they wished to convey as opposed to the sound that was generated.

On the sixth and final day, students were asked to focus on completing the image assortment and narration recording as a priority. As a final step, students were encouraged to include transitions and special effects adding motion, panning, scanning, and animation to their work. Students were regularly reminded to practice precision and economy in the placement of such effects as the emphasis needed to be on conveying meaning and thinking, not on demonstrating technological savvy. In fact, most students found the additional effects to be a distraction, employing little more than "fade" transitions or an occasional pan across an image.

RAI'S VISUAL THINK-ALOUD

Rai's work was built from both his "sparks" and the visual representations he created in order to depict his envisioned story world. Rai chose to focus on the first three pages of the text, mostly because he wanted to limit the length of the finished product. Further, he had generated many more "sparks" and notes than he'd anticipated and felt initially overwhelmed by the volume of his response. He wrote, "I don't read this much and think that I'll do more with a little bit of novel as opposed to forgetting sparks and just reading a whole lot. I have to think about reading instead of just reading."

The images in Rai's piece were all photographs that he gathered outside of class due to class time limits and his feeling that "class is about the reading." He saw representation as something separate from his close thinking about the text. Rai clearly struggled, uncertain about the process of creating a mental movie or envisioning text. Further, he felt blocked by his inability to draw or create an artistic representation. His journal entry after the third day expressed much of this frustration:

If I read more, maybe I'd get this. I feel like I'm creating pictures where they weren't happening. I see colors, sharp corners, words, letters and brief "flashes," not a long movie or something I can draw.

The requirement wasn't to be an artist but to represent the big ideas that stood out as students' read and visualized. Rai finally found momentum and comfort as he let go of the need to create realistic images and thought instead of representing what he actually envisioned. His resulting work was a combination of found art, original photographs, and collage. Rai's images all focused on one story component at a time, depicting fear, the voice, the airplane, and so on.

For example, Rai used a piece of abstract art (Rothko's "Untitled—1969") to represent his understanding and thinking about fear. He'd located an electronic copy of the image from the National Gallery of Art Web site, but thought of it when looking through an album of images taken by his family on a recent trip to Washington, D.C. Instead of including an image that contained physical objects that were either literal or figurative representations of fear for Rai, he chose the painting because of the colors it contained and the way in which Lowry's words had triggered his envisioned mental movie. He explained, "I matched the images to what went on in my head. I saw colors—cold colors—like in the painting. It feels empty, just like the main character in the novel. He can't even use his own words."

The visual think-aloud is a combination of sections from the novel read aloud, inserted comments reflecting Rai's "sparks" (the think-aloud), and a sequence of images representing his visualization. For example, the following table offers a sequence of images that appeared at the beginning of Rai's visual think-aloud alongside the text that he narrated (see Table 6.3). The image lingers on the screen, sometimes with a zoom or pan effect for motion, as Rai's voice narrates the text and offers the "sparks."

Rai spent a significant amount of time recording his narration, even though he had all of his notes and ideas planned out and practiced well in advance. As we discussed his progress at this point, he appeared to be blocked by the sound of his own voice. He'd rerecord a segment of the read-aloud multiple times, all of which sounded the same to both teachers. However, Rai clarified that it wasn't the sound of his voice that blocked his progress; it was the voice that he heard speaking. He explained, "I had to pay attention in a different way. Reading aloud slows me down and made me feel less smart. The think-aloud changed that by letting me hear myself as a reader."

TABLE 6.3: A PORTION OF RAI'S READ-ALOUD,
"SPARKS," AND VISUAL REPRESENTATIONS

OPENING TEXT FROM THE GIVER	RAI'S "SPARKS"	VISUAL REPRESENTATION	TEACHER NOTES *(recorded during a reflective discussion with Rai)*
It was almost December, and Jonas was beginning to feel frightened. No, wrong word, Jonas thought. Frightened meant that deep, sickening feeling of something terrible about to happen.	When I think of December, I get happy. It means snow, presents, and time with my Dad. Why scary?	Rai's representation of "fear." (An image of Rothko's "Untitled—1969" taken at the National Gallery of Art, Washington D.C.)	Dissonance here. Rai discusses happiness but represents fear. His explanation was that "what I thought in the spark came after what I saw." He is generating images before he stops to reflect on meaning and content.
Frightened was the way he had felt a year ago when an unidentified aircraft had overflown the community twice. He had seen it both times. Squinting toward the sky, he had seen the sleek jet, almost a blur at its high speed, go past, and a second later heard the blast of sound that followed. Then one more time, a moment later, from the opposite direction, the same plane.	I really don't like this. It reminds me of Sept. 11.	Rai's representation of fear, planes, and his connection— Sept. 11. (An image of an American flag.)	The description of the airplanes immediately led Rai to become locked on images related to what he remembered about 9–11. (A direct link between student experience and comprehension?) "When else did planes scare us?" "He says before that there was a 'deep, sickening feeling' just like what I remember." "I saw what I knew."

In reflecting about the process of constructing his visual think-aloud and those aspects that he might carry into later reading, Rai was much more confident and motivated. He wrote in his journal and handed me a written page (for emphasis) that said, "For the first time, I am going to finish a novel in English class." When I asked him about the technology he used, Rai explained "I needed to connect the pictures to my words and don't think that would have happened had we worked with just pictures or the (think-aloud) from earlier in the class. This helped me to see what I was supposed to be seeing as a reader all along."

NEXT STEPS

Screening and Discussion

The class shared and discussed the completed projects at the close of the work, reflecting on the effectiveness of the strategy, their work as readers, and what they understood as a result of the work that we had completed. The visual think-aloud activity was followed by additional direct instruction in reading strategies and teacher/student modeling of them, including prior knowledge activation, question generation, and summarization. I saw the visual think-aloud as an entrance for student readers into the work of an active, engaged reader. Subsequent strategies built from this base, again using technology only when it enhanced instructional goals. The project generated interesting findings in terms of Rai's engagement, visualization skills, work in elaborating on textual details, and overall participation in the classroom community.

Motivation

What was made clear in this work is that motivation has multiple aspects. Students began to develop their own goals for reading, generated in part by the tie to a novel that they self-selected. Rai explained after the visual think-aloud activity that "reading makes more sense now, and I know what I'm looking to do with the words on the page. It's more than that, and I like seeing the story happen." Rosenblatt explained that reading is an experience, and as teachers "our initial function is to deepen the experience . . . to return to, relive, and savor that experience (1982, p. 275). In this work, Rai began to do just that, experience and enjoy reading, and made subsequent gains in understanding as reflected in his response to and inferences about the text.

Rai's success in working with a self-selected text generated both intrinsic and extrinsic motivation in terms of classroom work. Rai began to regularly submit classwork, meet deadlines, and, perhaps more importantly, demonstrate close work in comprehending and understanding text. Further, the social community that developed in the classroom surrounding reading, the think-aloud process, and the development of the visual think-aloud provided another layer of motivation that led to an increase in Rai's self-efficacy. He began to ask fewer questions about the think-aloud process and more questions about key components of *The Giver.* Rai not only finished *The Giver,* but he continued to successfully work through the short story unit that followed.

Representation of Meaning

The images that students used to represent their story worlds provided students with visual texts to talk about and think with (Wilhelm 1995). Rai's reading visibly slowed as he considered his process and thinking, working hard to closely capture or develop effective, authentic representations. This was not an easy process, no matter how rich the end product. As Rai explained, "the picture had to be right in order for it all to make sense—and for the reading to be real to the viewer of my think-aloud." This reflected both the rigor of the process and one of its instructional values. Rai struggled because he was invested both in generating visualizations and in communicating that understanding and "seeing" to others.

Further, Rai generated the discourse, creating representations and envisionments that led to extensive, rich conversations about literary texts and the processes that he used as a reader. Here, "students have a concrete reference as they ask themselves and others: Why did you do that? What else can you do?" (Wilhelm 1995, p. 498). As Rai explained, "the pictures let me talk about what I was doing as a reader to figure out the book . . . It felt easier to get into the discussion and say something good."

Use of Reading Strategies

Within the construction of the visual think-aloud, Rai actively considered how meaning was built and conveyed both by the novel and by his representations and think-aloud. Strategies were deliberately practiced and invoked. He questioned coherence and continually reread, reinterpreted, and rearranged information. Where much of the preliminary work with the text (i.e., "sparks" and question development) provided the base for continued work, the visual think-aloud challenged Rai to compile and reconsider his ideas and responses in ways not seen within the verbal think-aloud process. Previously, Rai reported that he didn't visualize or generate a story world, let alone question, probe, and self-monitor as he read. Following this work, Rai's classroom comments in discussing literature spoke directly to generating visualizations and questioning texts while reading. He now records notes as he reads, going through stacks of sticky notes as he lists and reflects on his "sparks." His reader's journal contains sketches of scenes, visual representations of key vocabulary words, notes taken from his "sparks," and reflections on class discussion. A subsequent goal is for Rai to internalize these processes, without stopping to write out "sparks," refer to notes, or draw what he visualizes.

ENDING POINTS: TECHNOLOGY, LESSONS LEARNED, AND OTHER BIG IDEAS

Too often, researchers examine and write about a specific technology, not its use in classroom instruction. As Leu explains, "any new technology is not value-free; its integration or resistance will be determined largely by the values and practices of the teacher and organization in which it is placed" (2002, p. 758). In this case, we used visual tools to lead students to make visible a largely invisible practice. Students were able to use the basic, low-level technology to replicate a filmic mental movie and sequence those images with narrated text expressing their thoughts, responses, and questions as active readers. Though we could have used printed images accompanied by student performances of the think-aloud, it would have been at the cost of the filmic and at the cost of the "hook" provided by compelling, authentic work with powerful technology tools. Further, students identified and revised multiple instances when inferences didn't match the visual or verbal cues offered by the additional elements of the full product.

Not everything went as smoothly as anticipated, despite a significant amount of front-end structuring and preparation:

- It was challenging to ensure that students all had equal access to the classroom computers, especially since so few students had access to computers at home.
- Server space was an issue as the iMovie files tended to be much larger than the size limits on student folders.
- Students needed to continually be reminded to save their work, with two students losing full class periods of work when the network crashed or programs locked.
- Time was limited, as we faced curricular coverage needs and missed instructional time due to inclement weather.

The project was more effective when students used iMovie as the digital video tool, which allowed for a seamless flow of images alongside two audio tracks. Those students who used iMovie demonstrated increased understanding of the differences between reading aloud and thinking aloud. Further, those students who used iMovie and had previously reported that they lacked a mental movie when reading, self-reported significantly more visualization and envisionments as they worked through subsequent texts. They explained that iMovie "generated an actual movie with flow as opposed to a series of PowerPoint slides that were more clunky."

It was also important to note that the intuitive nature of the tools encouraged students to be more willing to revise or make corrections to the reading of the visual think-aloud. Several students reread, reinterpreted, and reorganized previously represented material after viewing their draft products and considering both coherence and connection to the original text.

Big Ideas for the Classroom

This project revealed the following elements of an effective and rigorous visualization task:

- The task should lead students to evoke the story world.
- The task should encourage students to reread and reconsider their understanding both to develop a richer reading and to reflect on their reading process.
- The task should be compelling, fun, and require that students work beyond skills that they have already mastered.
- The task should involve some sort of "real" work that has meaning beyond the classroom.

The "So What" of It All . . .

Perhaps one of the most exciting things about considering what rich, meaningful technology integration can introduce into our classrooms is the fact that we do not really know what is yet to come or how it will impact our work. As teachers, we are continually learning instructional best practices. The trick is to know how to take advantage of the unique capacities of a technology tool to do something that is more powerful than what we did without it.

In the case of the visual think-aloud, Rai was able to use the technology tools to see how a reader can work with text. He was able to experience the construction of his visualized mental movie. He was able to see those moments when a reader steps in and out of the print text, questioning, analyzing, commenting, and connecting. As he explained in a journal entry, "I made the invisible, visible." He made significant gains in terms of motivation, understanding of what readers' work actually involves, confidence, and self-monitored use of specifically selected reading strategies. Where this activity didn't fill in all the holes in his background or lead to a complete change in his reading behavior or work as a student, it provided him with a successful starting point. He willingly enters assigned class texts and is less hesitant and less likely to stop reading at the first sign of trouble. He knows a handful of moves that he can make to understand and then apply what he learns from what he reads. It isn't an automatic fix, but he offers in discussion, "I know that I can do it when I'm willing to work, ask, and participate. Me, I learned that reading is seeing and then starting to know—not just knowing from the start."

7: Making Meaning

In preparation for my assignment to "cover" for a colleague's tenth-grade English class (three days into the fall term), I dipped into my folder of favorites, almost holding my breath while anticipating stepping into a fresh classroom and working with a tried and true "friend" of an activity. Working with a stack of copies of a short story we were to read, I chose to open class by asking students to do what Berthoff (1980) refers to as "noticing what you notice," taking note of what is interesting, what questions the text generates, what you want to speak against, and so on.

We were reading Atwood's "Bread," a short story with so many layers, I was convinced we could easily spend the entire class period in a lively discussion of its many possibilities. Twenty minutes ticked by quickly as students read the story, and a few appeared to be, in some way, marking up the text. After an additional ten minutes, I noted little more progress, and opened the floor for discussion. Nothing. Thinking that it was just the newness of my presence in the room, I offered a question that had grown from my own reading. Still nothing. Some kids were looking around the room; some kids were staring nervously down at their desks, clearly anticipating that I'd begin calling on individual students to offer their thoughts. I waited. And waited.

Finally, just as I thought all was lost, Mike offered what I'd hoped to be the insight to get the ball rolling . . .

"So, I know that this is wrong and all, but she kept saying 'you, you, you' but she switched it up with the paragraphs. I didn't write anything down because she ejected me."

A resounding nodding of heads and hands chorused across the classroom.

"Ok, tell me more," I prompted.

"So, you've got a person eating bread and I'm all into that . . . but the same dude is starving and then in prison. Then, I'm lost. Just tell me what it means."

I wish that I could capture the frustration in Joshua's voice as he spoke that last sentence. It wasn't resigned. It wasn't detached. It was angry. And he wasn't the only one.

"Your question to us is good and all, but it didn't tell me where to go. I feel played, and I don't want to. The writer played me good, but that don't mean nothing but I don't know what happened," vented Martika.

"Why should I even keep reading once the story shifts like that? I just didn't," offered Chuck.

"I skipped ahead to the last line of the story . . . 'You don't want to know, imagine that.' I'm not imagining that. I'm there. I don't want to know because she left me hanging after that first paragraph," explained Lucy.

We talked a great deal about how the paragraphs of the story were working together and apart—and what the students saw as a deceptive character that wasn't them and wasn't holding the story together. Thirty-seven of the thirty-nine students in the classroom acknowledged that they hadn't taken marginal notes or written what they'd noticed because they shut down as readers once the story broke with convention. They felt that there was nothing to "notice" past that point because they didn't know what to do as readers.

"You don't mess with character, man," offered Rody. "When she messed with that, she messed with the thing that kept me in it. If I'm seeing through eyes, you got to keep them."

We spent the entire block period talking through Atwood's story, possibilities for the identity of "you," possibilities for why the story would offer a variety of perspectives and lenses through which we could peer as readers, and the complexities of the moves she'd made as a writer. I walked a delicate line between offering my reading and providing space for theirs. However, bigger than the story were our discoveries about how this class was working as readers.

"So, when we read in here, isn't there something specific we are each supposed to know?" asked Chuck.

"I'm not reading to imagine or envision or whatever your word was. I'm reading to get the stuff . . . the info. There is business to be done here," explained Joshua.

We talked about the difference between what the class saw as school reading and reading that they engaged in outside of class.

"Here, I've got to take the test. That means there is something that I've got to get into the text and find. That's how I read in school. I don't read to get swept away. I read to pass," offered Javon.

"I don't like reading things that are on this copy paper," explained Shelby. "I want the questions and vocabulary words so I know what to think. In here, it's about getting the answer and getting to lunch. Right?"

When the bell rang, we'd uncovered much about the complexities of Atwood's story and how they could work as readers to construct meaning. However, as much as I'd tried to build a space for a different kind of reading in this class, students resisted. They were looking to read for an answer that they expected the text to deliver.

BIG IDEAS: READING, READER RESPONSE, AND THE VISUAL

As I left period four and made my way down the hall, I was overrun by thoughts about reading, reading theory, curriculum, and schooling. Clearly, these were students who were well-skilled in what Rosenblatt called "efferent reading" (1978). In-school reading was about finding information or reading the text to get something specific from it. Reading wasn't as I wanted to see it framed, as "aesthetic experience" or the reader's evocation of the text as it is imagined and visualized and experienced in the mind's eye. To that end, the sticky note clinging to my screen reads:

> *Students read literature to know themselves, and, insofar as they each are a composite of their ideas, attitudes, beliefs, and emotions, to create themselves, for reading will enable them to refine and sharpen their conceptions of the world and the people in it. (Probst 2005, p. 31)*

This isn't the kind of reading that was happening in period four. Instead, students were making the critical assumption that their responses to the text would be meaningless or riddled with errors. They wanted the answer to write in their notebooks. And they were so accustomed to this that they couldn't see into a task that asked them to step out and think.

I want my students to experience something very different. I want them to abandon the idea that the meaning exists solely in the text, or, at the opposite end of the pendulum, solely in their own minds. Instead, I want them to see that a reader brings a unique set of experiences and understandings (prior knowledge), an understanding of how texts work (text type knowledge), and a set of procedures or strategies that when deployed will help them to engage with the text.

Smokey Daniels, speaking in a session at the Walloon Institute in 2003, provided me with the dominant way in which I now see reading in my classroom. He simply explained that "texts need to function as mirrors and as windows; the mirror allows students to see and discover parts of who they are, and the window challenges them to see beyond their known place and experience." Amen, Smokey.

As my dominant metaphor for thinking about reading is visual, it follows that I use multiple visual strategies to lead students to engage with print text in such a way that they look both within and outside of themselves. The visual strategies I use encourage students to access and apply prior knowledge as they read, to increase comprehension, and to predict, infer, and even remember what they read. Bottom line—readers matter here. It matters what they bring to the text. It matters what they see. It matters what they take away. My goal is to select texts that they can connect to and learn from; to equip them with skills, strategies, and motivation; and then to support, facilitate, and often get out of the way. I want my students to see and to be seen.

INTO THE CLASSROOM

What follows are strategies that allow students to enter into some sophisticated ideas in literary study: character, plot, setting, theme, figurative language, denouement. Again, the same principles are in play here that lived in earlier chapters. The strategies provide a visual way into the texts that we read. Students enter texts, construct envisionments, communicate meaning using multiple modes and media, and respond.

Character Journal

This is a strategy that I remember from my own experiences as a student in Mrs. Lucas' eleventh-grade English class. Midway through the semester, we started reading *The Great Gatsby,* and, as we were growing tired of our response journaling, she asked us to switch gears. Instead of writing through our lens as readers, we would write from the point of view of one of the characters in the novel. I was challenged to look through Myrtle's eyes and make meaning of both the events in the novel and her own moments of introspection.

In working with my own students, I've used this strategy with multiple literary texts and at multiple grade levels. The only real constants in the assignment over the years have been that students need to stay with a single character over the course of the novel, and that the product needs to be a journal that looks as if it were in the possession of that character. Although I have sometimes assigned particular characters to students, I've had the best results when students select characters, usually noting their choice on a sign-up sheet we quickly pass around at the end of a class. Sometimes, I've been surprised by the choices. For example, one of the most insightful journals I've seen was written by Sharon, an eighth-grade student who chose to see through the eyes of the cat in *Animal Farm*. Its cover is shown in Figure 7.1.

FIGURE 7.1:
SHARON'S CHARACTER JOURNAL

We still work with pens, paper, and physical materials like the mouse on the front cover of Sharon's journal. Some students have gone high-tech, using flash to create an animated, narrated journal or creating an extensive Web site. The caution I give them throughout the task is that the technology should not interfere with the content and inferences that the journal offers. The rule-of-thumb in my classroom is that the use of technology is encouraged so long as it adds to the intended meaning of the product. So, for students who were maintaining journals as we read *1984* or *Feed*, technology became an option— but only insofar as students could support their choices.

Open Minds

The open mind strategy asks students to construct a visual representation of both a text and the student's reading of it. Figure 7.2 is an example of an open

FIGURE 7.2:
RACHEL'S OPEN MIND

mind constructed by Rachel as she read Yeats's "Second Coming." Where a traditional open mind in my class asks students to graphically "fill" a sketch of a human head, Rachel wanted to use her skills with Photoshop to create a visual representation where "the bounds are those within the printed page as those were the only bounds to what I saw as happening within the poem."

It's essential that, though these are visual texts, they are accompanied by written reflections and arguments that explain the components of the visual text and the print text that cued them. In my classroom, I look for a "meaty" written analysis with more depth than would have likely been seen had the student not completed the visual component of the task.

When I use this strategy, it's usually done throughout the reading of a rich, compelling text. Instead of asking students to quickly jot down a sketch, I encourage them to take time, and to allow the reading to inform the graphic just as the graphic begins to play into the reading. In Rachel's case, this was a piece that went through eleven revisions, which she explained was ten more than any solely written text she submitted in class. She offered, "Each time I'd work on the image, I found myself rereading the poem, and bigger than that, rethinking the poem. With words, I tend to think that what's down is it. Here, I felt like the image was a bigger statement than what I might just write."

Graphic Notes

I firmly believe that my students need a variety of tools through which they can construct meaning and organize their thinking about a class text. To that end, I supply a series of options, some designed using Inspiration software (visual), some using 3×5 cards (textual), and still others using podcasts and audio blog posts (auditory). My current favorite graphic organizer for graphic note-taking was developed by Jim Burke (available at www.englishcompanion.com).

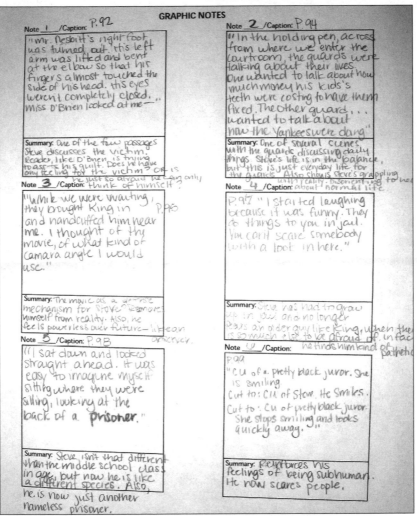

A considerable majority of my students are taken aback when I ask them to record visual response notes or to record their understanding from reading a piece of nonfiction using a storyboard. They argue that English class isn't art class, and that drawing is for students in younger grades. Some stay resolute, filling the boxes with words (see Figure 7.3), while others enjoy the opportunity to exercise their graphic skills (see Figure 7.4). The unexpected turnaround that happens for most of my students occurs

FIGURE 7.4: "ARTISTIC" GRAPHIC NOTES OF DEATH OF A SALESMAN

when they realize (usually without my prompting) that this is drawing to think.

Pat's graphic notes (Figure 7.5) were recorded as he reread a section of *Monster* which he found to be particularly challenging. As he worked, he noted his progress in his class journal:

I don't know what it is about this assignment, but I have never taken so much time to read something before. I think it's because I'm taking time to allow the pictures to unfold in my head. Usually, I'm quicker than that, and when I don't understand, I skip over to a part where I do. This is a little risky, but if I'm wrong, at least I have something to fall back on.

Not only do students tend to read deliberately and reread more often during this assignment, they also tend to jump eagerly into classroom discussion. Our discussions have ranged from ways in which images represent words to ways that a writer's words can evoke different images to different readers— conversations that involve many more students than when we depend on different forms of response and notetaking.

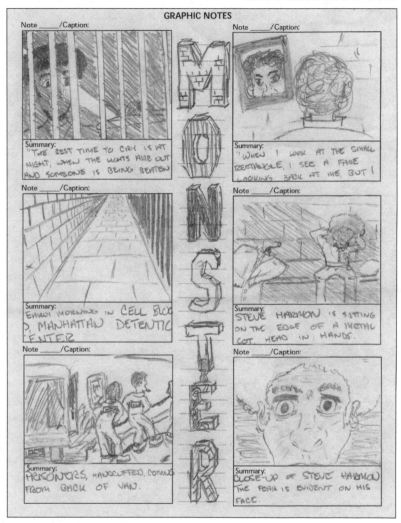

Two-Minute Movies

This strategy begins with what my students call "reader's questions." To use their words, these are the questions that result "when in thinking about what I read, I stumble into something new" (Lindsay, grade 8) or when "in reading something starts to stir that I need to puzzle out"(Delphi, grade 11). Students formulate a question that they want to use the text to pursue, sometimes as a group and sometimes as an individual.

MANAGING
THE TECHNOLOGY

Where resources for use with blogs are being developed faster than this book can stay timely, there are some guiding questions to consider when working with blogging tools.

1. *Does the new capacity or function allow students to communicate clearly and concisely?*

2. *Are there several steps to getting the tool to work? Or, can you teach with the tool without having to teach the tool?*

3. *How readily do you want students to make postings? What kinds of postings will be most appropriate?*

4. *Do you need parental or even administrative permissions in order to require that students have fairly constant access to their blogs?*

5. *Do you want to make the blogs public or private? Are there building or system policies for that?*

For more on Web logs (and the tools to use with them for multimodal publishing), see the companion Web site for this book at www. bringingtheoutsidein.com.

The video that students construct is a visual and narrated attempt at "answering" their questions. Instead of using video to enact and record scenes, students do something called "pause editing," holding images or posting them on the wall, recording while they read text from a written script, and then pausing the camera until they raise or hang the next image. These images are constructed from cut-up magazines, original art, or original photography printed from the class printer. The finished product is a two-minute video that is as compelling and rich as the script and images allow.

Rachel, an enthusiastic, even hungry, ninth-grade reader explained this strategy as:

> *The first time that I was able to make my words and pictures work as reading tools. Yeah, we did the graphic notes and stuff, but that was more of my pictures working after the words had worked on me. With this, it's the author's words working with my pictures and my words. I understand in a completely different way.*

Her two-minute movie used *Monster* and addressed whether or not Miss Petrocelli believed in Steve's innocence. Her voice narrated the following lines as images of clouds, and then handcuffs, and then a jail cell appeared on the screen, each built from paint, scraps of paper, and pieces of metal:

> *As much as we might describe ourselves as innocent, the meaning of that word doesn't hold unless it's given to us by someone else. Instead, it comes from outside, from others. Miss Petrocelli labels Steve by her actions, but she never uses the word.*

The reflective paper accompanying her work identified this six-second clip as the point where she began to understand the relationship between these two characters. She wrote:

> *Before really thinking about this, I didn't link the two of them beyond just the fact that she was his lawyer. I didn't get why he cared so much. But if he can't own that word, it makes this so much bigger. Wow.*

One note about copyright . . . I require that students create a "works cited" page that offers an annotated bibliography of the sources used in the movie. It's all too often that my students seem to believe that if they got it from a Web site or they cut it out of a magazine, it's theirs. We talk extensively about the use of a text (whether it's visual, auditory, or in print) and the value of intellectual property.

Photoblogs and Vlogs

Quite literally, had I written this same section one month ago, I would be discussing how students used weblogs to maintain written journals in response to the texts that we read. My argument for how this was a visual form of communication had to do with design and form of written posts. In the period of one month, this has all changed—which makes me wonder what will be possible by the time this book is in your hands.

A Web log is, in it's simplest form, an online journal. Several years ago, the few blogs that existed on the Web were essentially online journals, most of which served as filters of Web content on a single topic. A strength that continues is that most allowed commentary from readers, providing a collaborative space connecting readers and writers across the globe.

Two big things happened to change that history. First, blogger.com, a free tool that allowed users to publish blogs without knowing any html coding, was bought out by google.com, the most powerful and possibly most accessed search engine. Now, a major blog-creating tool was available to the masses, and being supported and developed. Second, journalists started to take advantage of the medium. Suddenly, the *Washington Post,* the *New York Times,* ESPN, the "Today Show" . . . all had blogs that first and foremost provided information and, secondly, provided models for what the common blogger could do.

In my classroom, I learned about blogs from my students. Most notably, these weren't students who were hungry writers in the English classroom.

However, in their lives outside of class, they were prolific posters to both their own blogs and those of their peers (and beyond as they responded to the postings of authors, politicians, artists, musicians, and whomever else they took issue with or supported). Then, they started to teach me about features of blogs I hadn't yet seen. Using blogger.com, they could make a thirty-second audio posting by calling a 1–800 number at the site. Using blogger.com and a Web tool available at flickr.com, they could post images to their blogs. Then, blogger. com developed a tool to allow students to post from Microsoft Word. And, to quote Malcolm Gladwell, things tipped . . .

When it comes to the use of technology tools in my English classroom, I require that the tool must allow us to do something better than what we could have accomplished without it. We had that in blogs. Further, when taking advantage of the graphical capabilities of the tools, journaling online can now include images, video, and sound. Add in the capacity for collaborative comments and posting, and the possibilities for composing with blogs in the English classroom seem almost without bounds. These additional capacities are powerful and readily used enough to have launched two new descriptors—photoblogs and vlogs. It's important to note that these aren't new genres; they are descriptions of what is delivered textually. So, a photoblog offers images where a vlog offers video.

Using blogger.com and two additional tools (www.flickr.com for image posting and Serious Magic software for video posting), students can now create online journals that use image and video postings to communicate their understanding of the texts they read in rich, compelling ways. For example, students could use blogs to house class tableaux depicting scenes and vocabulary words, or to post written and even visual essays that offer recasting of scenes or rewritten endings to the novels. Others might want to use these tools to house a character journal or "digital yearbook."

ENDING POINTS

Reading is interactive. Reading is about constructing meaning. Reading is about deploying specific, deliberate strategies meant to help a reader make sense of a text. Reading is purposeful. These are my "non-negotiables" when it comes to how I want my students to understand their work as readers, and how I want to work as a reader, myself.

Working within that framework, the readers in my classroom are asked to visualize as they read, and to create and use visual tools to organize content, construct meaning, and analyze their processes and understanding. So many of the tools and tasks described in this chapter are about using visual tools to get meaning down into a form that can be interpreted and further analyzed. Just as the texts we read function as Smokey Daniels's windows and mirrors, so do my students' visual response texts.

This isn't just a collection of tools that are meant to scaffold struggling readers into rich texts, though that is a part of the work. It's also about leading even highly-able readers to read more challenging texts with greater facility. Or, as Matt explained after completing a character journal for class, "it's about your seeing me, and my ways of thinking, and my being strong when I go into a text." Exactly. Welcome to the literacy club.

Afterword: Seeing Again

> *Old paint on canvas, as it ages, sometimes becomes transparent.*
> *When that happens, it is possible, in some pictures, to see the*
> *original lines: a tree will show through a woman's dress, a*
> *child makes way for a dog, a large boat is no longer on an*
> *open sea . . . Perhaps it would be as well to say that the old*
> *conception, replaced by a later choice, is a way of seeing and*
> *then seeing again. (Hellman 1973, p. 3)*

Revisiting Rai and Gus's classroom at the end of the academic year, I found myself surprised not only by the ways in which the students had grown (and not grown) as readers and writers, but by the ways in which my thinking as a literacy teacher had changed. Our work was about their discovery (and rediscovery) of their literacy skills as readers and writers, but it was also my path into, through, and within what I believed and valued about student reading, writing, and thinking.

Gus found me in the hall a few days after we'd completed the last in a series of visual think-alouds while reading Camus's *The Stranger*. He thrust a paper into my hands as I juggled a stack of papers and books, precariously balanced and tottering just enough to lead him to snicker that I was the techie-teacher . . . We walked into the classroom and I asked him what he was giving me. He responded, "what reading looks like," bringing me back full circle to the first conversation that we'd shared several months ago.

As I read the quotation, he appeared to be ready to jump out of his skin.

"Tell me more," I prompted.

"We read this in art class—but I think it's about reading. First, I thought it was about the think-alouds and how you have all those layers to what a reader does, but it's bigger. See, I read now in here," he said as he pointed around our classroom walls.

"What I used to think about reading is like the pencil sketch that is underneath the painting. What I hear and see when I read provides some of the layers, and I'm adding layers all the time when I figure out something new, or something happens that changes the me that is doing the reading. To me, this is real reading. And I finally see what it looks like."

Our conversation didn't last long as the class was filling with students and Gus, a typical tenth-grade boy, didn't want to be seen demonstrating overt enthusiasm about reading. I was overwhelmed with things I wanted to discuss with Gus about the quote, his insights, his growth in the class. And I was so struck by the differences in the Gus I'd known and the Gus I'd come to see.

Would it have been easy for Gus to sit back and perform his earlier "strategies" for earning his B in class? Absolutely. I firmly believe that had we not taken what felt like a risk and brought the multiple and nuanced literacies that my students thrived on outside of our classroom into our work together that Gus would have continued on that path. By looking at ways those literacies could allow us to make reading and thinking visible, we were able to figure out where each student was and where we needed to go to get to the next point in becoming more successful with the literacies that were seen in the conventional classroom.

Writing our story has challenged me to see again not only the leaps that students were able to make, but another reality as well. As powerful as these strategies were in providing students with entrances into our work as thoughtful, deliberate readers and writers, their greatest strength was their ability to lead students to exercise their literacies—and be seen within an English/Language Arts curriculum that typically didn't acknowledge their non-school literacies.

When I read the quote Gus gave me through my teacher lens, I quickly see that my thinking as a teacher is just as layered as the painting. It has changed as my understanding of literacy and how students read has changed, continually influenced by colleagues and students. I'm still learning. There are students whom I haven't found a way to engage. That said, Rai, Dahabo, Gus, and all the students in this book have made such a strong impact on my thinking and teaching that I expect their lessons to rise through and shape the layers that come next.

This book is far from exhaustive when it comes to the multiple strategies that can be put into play through the smart, effective use of the unique capacities of multimodal tools to lead students to engage with print texts. I think of them more as seeds, ideas that lead to other possibilities. My goal has been to provide you with models and voices that can help you see your students and classroom in what's discussed here, and to provide tools that lead you and your students to engage more deeply and more closely in your work together. Ultimately, it is an invitation to examine, play, invent, reinvent, and join in the conversation.

REFERENCES

Allen, J. 1999. *Words, Words, Words.* Portland, ME: Stenhouse.

Alliance for Excellent Education. 2003. *Left Out and Behind: NCLB and the American High School.* Washington, D.C.

Allington, R. 2006. *What Really Matters for Struggling Readers.* 2nd ed. Boston, MA: Pearson.

Anderson, L. H. 2001. *Speak.* New York: Puffin.

Atwell, N. 1998. *In the Middle,* 2nd ed. Portsmouth, NH: Heinemann.

Beck, I., M. McKeown, and L. Kucan. 2002. *Bringing Words to Life: Robust Vocabulary Instruction.* New York: Guilford Press.

Beers, K. 2002. *When Kids Can't Read, What Teachers Can Do: A Guide for Teachers 6–12.* Portsmouth, NH: Heinemann.

———— 2003. "When Students Struggle with Writing and Reading." Presentation delivered at National Council of Teachers of English National Conference.

Berthoff, A. 1980. *The Making of Meaning: Metaphors, Models, and Maxims for Writing Teachers.* NJ: Boynton Cook.

Betts, E. A. 1996. *Foundations of Reading Instruction.* New York: American Book Company.

Biancarosa, G., and C. Snow. 2004. *Reading Next: A Vision for Action and Research in Middle and High School Literacy.* Washington, DC: Alliance for Excellent Education.

Blachowicz, C. L. Z., and P. Fisher, 2000. "Vocabulary Instruction." In M. L. Kamil, P. B. Mosenthal, P. D. Pearson and R. Barr, eds., *Handbook of Reading Research: Vol. 3,* pp. 503–523. Mahwah, NJ: Lawrence Erlbaum.

Bomer, K. 2005. *Writing a Life: Teaching Memoir to Sharpen Insight, Shape Meaning—and Triumph Over Tests.* Portsmouth, NH: Heinemann.

Bruner, J. 1986. *Actual Minds, Possible Worlds.* Cambridge, MA: Harvard University Press.

Burke, J. 1995. *I Hear America Reading.* Portsmouth, NH: Heinemann.

——— 2002. *Tools for Thought: Graphic Organizers for Your Classroom.* Portsmouth, NH: Heinemann.

Daniels, H. 2003. *Literature Circles: Voice and Choice in Book Clubs and Reading Groups,* 2nd ed. Portland, ME: Stenhouse.

——— 2003. "This Stupid Job!" Keynote delivered at the Walloon Institute, Lake Geneva, WI.

De Leon, A. 2002. *The Urban High School's Challenge: Ensuring Literacy for Every Child.* New York: Carnegie Corporation of New York.

Donahue, P., M. Daane and W. Grigg. 2003. *The Nation's Report Card: Reading Highlights, 2003.* Washington, DC: National Center for Education Statistics.

Duke, N., and D. Pearson. 2002. "Effective Practices for Developing Reading Comprehension." In A. E. Farstrup, ed., *What Research Has to Say about Reading Instruction.* Newark, DE: International Reading Association.

Dyson, A. H. 1999. "Transforming Transfer: Unruly Children, Contrary Texts and the Persistence of the Pedagogical Order." *Review of Research in Education* 24: 141–171.

Dyson, A., and C. Genishi. 1994. *The Need for Story: Cultural Diversity in the Classroom and Community.* Urbana, IL: National Council of Teachers of English.

Friere, P., and D. Macedo. 1987. *Literacy: Reading the Word and the World.* South Hadley, MA: Bergin & Garvey.

Gallas, K. 2003. *Imagination and Literacy: A Teacher's Search for the Heart of Learning.* New York: Teachers College Press.

Gee, J. P. 2004. *Situated Language and Learning: A Critique of Traditional Schooling.* New York: Routledge.

Graves, M., and S. Watts-Taffe 2002. "The Place of Word Consciousness in a Research-Based Vocabulary Program." In A. Farstrup and S. J. Samuels, eds. *What the Research Has to Say about Reading Instruction*, pp. 140–165. Newark, DE: International Reading Association.

Greene, M. 2003. *Releasing the Imagination: Essays on Education, the Arts, and Social Change.* San Francisco, CA: Jossey Bass.

Harvey, S., and A. Goudvis. *Strategies that Work.* Portland, ME: Stenhouse.

Heard, G., *The Revision Toolbox.* Portsmouth, NH: Heinemann.

Heath, S. B. 2000. "Seeing Our Way into Learning." *Cambridge Journal of Education,* 30 (1): 121–132.

Hellman, L. 1973. *Pentimento: A Book of Portraits.* Boston: Little, Brown.

Ivey, G. "A Multi-case Study in Middle School: Complexities Among Young Adolescent Readers." *Reading Research Quarterly* 34: 172–192.

Jerry, L., and A. Lutkus. 2003. *The Nation's Report Card: Reading Highlights from the NAEPs, 2002: 2002 Reading Trends Differ by Grades.* NCES.

Keene, E. L., and S. Zimmerman. 1997. *Mosaic of Thought: Teaching Comprehension in a Reader's Workshop.* Portsmouth, NH: Heinemann.

Kress, G. 2003. *Literacy in the New Media Age.* New York: Routledge Press.

Lambert, J. 2002. *Digital Storytelling: Capturing Lives, Creating Community.* Berkeley: Digital Diner.

Langer, J. 1995. *Envisioning Literature: Literary Understanding and Literature Instruction.* New York: Teachers College.

Lave and Wenger. 1991. *Situated Learning: Legitimate Peripheral Participation.* New York: Cambridge University Press.

Leu, D. 2002. "Literacy & Technology: Deitic Consequences for Literacy Education in an Information Age." In M. Kamil, P. B. Mosenthal, P. D. Pearson, & R. Barr, eds., *Handbook of Reading Research*, pp. 743–70. Mahwah, NJ: Erlbaum & Assoc.

Luke, A., and J. Elkins. 2000. "Re/mediating Adolescent Literacies." *Journal of Adolescent and Adult Literacy,* 43: 396–398.

Martin, S. 1998. "The Hundred Greatest Books That I've Read." *The New Yorker*, 74:148.

Mavers, D. 2003. "Communicating Meanings Through Image Composition." In C. Jewitt and G. Kress, eds., *Multimodal Literacy.* New York: Peter Lang Publishing.

McKenna, M. 2004. "Teaching Vocabulary to Struggling Older Readers." *Perspectives,* 30 (1): 13–16.

Moss, G. 2003. "Putting the Text Back into Practice." In J. Jewitt & G. Kress, eds., *Multimodal Literacy.* New York: Peter Lang Publishing.

Myers, M. 1996. *Changing Our Minds: Negotiating English and Literacy.* Urbana, IL: NCTE.

Nagy, W. 1988. *Teaching Vocabulary to Improve Reading Comprehension.* Newark, DE: International Reading Association.

National Center for Education Statistics. 2003. *The Nation's Report Card 2002.* Retrieved from http://nces.ed.gov.

National Endowment for the Arts. 2004. *Reading at Risk: A Survey of Literary Reading in America.* Research Division Report #46. Washington, DC: National Endowment for the Arts.

New London Group. 1996. "A Pedagogy of Multiliteracies". *Harvard Educational Review*, 66 (1): 60–92.

Probst, R. 2005. *Response and Analysis: Teaching Literature in Secondary School.* Portsmouth, NH: Heinemann.

Quindlen, A. 1998. *How Reading Changed My Life*. New York: Ballantine Books.

Rich, A. 1979. *On Lies, Secrets, and Silence: Selected Prose.* Chicago: W. W. Norton.

Roorbach, B. 1998. *Writing Life Stories.* Chicago: Story.

Rosenblatt, L. 1978. *The Reader, the Text, the Poem: A Transactional Theory of the Literary Work.* Carbondale, IL: Southern Illinois Press.

——— 1982. "The Literary Transaction: Evocation and Response". *Theory into Practice* 21: 268–277.

Steineke, N. 2001. *Reading and Writing Together: Collaborative Literacy in Action.* Portsmouth, NH: Heinemann.

Tovani, C. 2004. *Do I Really Have to Teach Reading?* Portland, ME: Stenhouse.

Wilhelm, J. D. 1995. "Reading Is Seeing: Using Visual Response to Improve the Literary Reading of Reluctant Readers." *Journal of Reading Behavior* 27 (4): 467–503.

Wilhelm, J. D., T. N. Baker, and J. Dube. 2001. *Strategic Reading: Guiding Students to Lifelong Literacy, 6–12.* Portsmouth, NH: Heinemann.

Yardley, J. 1998. "The List of Great Novels: Read It and Weep." *The Washington Post,* July 28, p. D02.